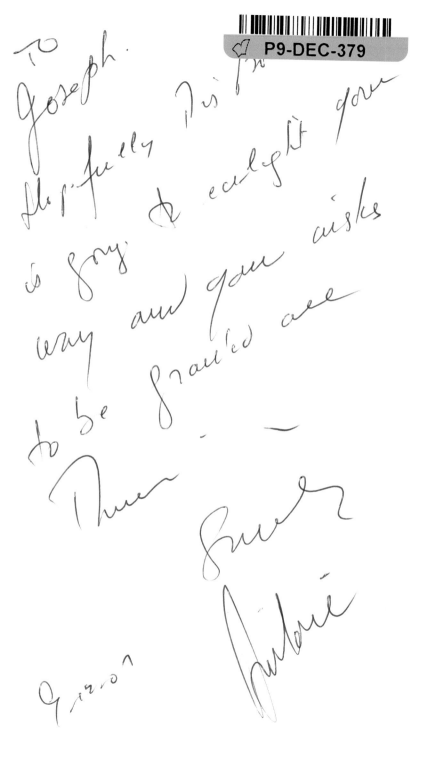

To
Joseph.

Hopefully This
is going to enlighten your
way and your wishes
to be granted all
Dream

Best

Simone

Girven

"The thought of love is consistent and it never changes. However, you always have a different thought opposing peace because you are not in the mind of love. You travel in time with your thoughts. You are amused with your thoughts, but none of them are part of your truth. You believe your thoughts are for and of your goodness, but in fact, your own thoughts are the cause of your pain and unhappiness. The thought of love is your real thought, the only thought that provides goodness to you."

COGITO:

Cogito ergo sum: *I think therefore, I am*.

Cogito ergo sum: *Je pense, done je suis*

COGITO

Part 1

Antoine & Liliana

The Separation

AJL

Publishers

AJL Publishers

Title: Cogito, Part 1: Antoine and Liliana, The Separation

Authors: Antoine Bacha and Liliana Franco

www.cogitobook.com

We dedicate this book to all who are besieged by the questions and contradictions that arise in the course of human life. We hope that you will receive the words written here in the same spirit in which we received them and now pass on to you. We feel very deeply that the more you read and ponder these thoughts, the more you will understand – just as we did.

To all, with love,

Antoine Bacha
Liliana Franco

Chapter One

On one day in 1982, high above the earth, a flight between Athens and Paris fell victim to hijackers.

Flight Engineer Antoine Bacha heard a commotion coming from the passengers' cabin. He unbuckled himself from his station in the cockpit to see what was going on.

As he opened the door to the passenger cabin, he was shocked to see a man viciously battering a female passenger. Antoine's first instinct was to lunge at the attacker to save the woman, but during the fight, he was knocked unconscious by a blow to the head.

Often, our first inclination when we see someone in distress is to help. However, action without forethought often yields unpredictable results just as it can for many of us who act impulsively - before thinking. For Antoine, his actions had put his life in jeopardy. His chances of survival now hung by a thread.

Days later, Antoine would awaken in Lebanon in a small cave-like hole measuring approximately two feet by two feet, and not much more than that in depth. This is where Antoine lived, as a prisoner of Lebanese terrorists for nine months and sixteen days, confined to a small hole in the ground wearing nothing but his underwear.

It was to be a life of horror as the terrorists began to torture and beat Antoine. They ripped his fingernails from his hands with pliers. This man was a commercial pilot, he was neither a CIA agent nor an agent of the FBI, and yet they interrogated him using the most extreme, inhuman and vicious methods, accusing him of being a government spy.

The way the terrorists beat him, it was amazing that Antoine did not lapse into unconsciousness or even death from the pain. The beatings and actions of these men were those of determined murderers. Their intentions were clearly to make their captives wish for death rather than to endure life in captivity.

Then one day, within the chaotic atmosphere and the barbarism of the terrorists, something extraordinary happened; something that usually only individuals of strong faith can accept or relate to. That little miracle that we seldom think of as a miracle often results in a most remarkable thing: it enables us to finally discover who we really are. The endless torture forced Antoine to learn how to focus his mind and discover the truth of the 'inner-self'.

Antoine may have not believed in miracles prior to this encounter. Certainly, he learned to believe in something while tucked tightly in that ghastly prison. In the face of overwhelming emotional strain, it took extreme anger and desperation to make him stop his racing thoughts, to calm his mind and to seek instead, inner peace. Antoine now shares his unique experience with the world. His miracle has opened a new door to his mind.

Time had passed slowly over those next three months. Even though the battering was horrible, paradoxically, Antoine experienced a strange kind of comfort. This strange comfort would keep him from going insane, and in the end, leave him unfazed by the events that overtook him.

We take for granted that our mind is real. And, we may assume that we do not have a spirit. (On the other hand, we may ask, "What is real?") Many things proven by the masters of 'Science' are difficult to believe. For centuries, men have questioned the capacity of the mind: what is myth, and what is fact? Research infers that if we used even only one fourth of our mind we would be considered extraordinarily intelligent. But in fact, we use far less than ten percent of our mind. In our lifetimes, there is no doubt that we could definitely utilize far more of the mind than we do.

Nonetheless, in the circumstances that Antoine found himself, one would predict that death would have been the certain outcome, but it was not. He was overwhelmed with anger but could do nothing but hope that one day he could take revenge. The pain was horrific, and the loathsome characters that inflicted his pain were without mercy. He thought to himself, "If I can only live another day…"

It was as Antoine struggled to stay alive, on the verge of giving up while in his dark hole, that the miracle appeared. He heard a voice. He didn't know where the voice came from, but, it was a voice that comforted him and soothed him. The voice told him that it would teach him. And it did. It taught Antoine about the powers of the mind:

"Understand that you are a mind and not a body. Your freedom will depend on your acceptance."

Antoine, crouched in his tiny dirt prison, couldn't see and he couldn't move, but he could still listen. The voice's message sounded simple enough. With nothing to lose, he seized the idea. He was certainly not going anywhere. Perhaps something could come of it.

Most would be full of fear, desperately seeking to claw their way to freedom, wasting valuable energy screaming and crying out, but Antoine began to listen. Most would not have taken this as calmly, hearing words from a disembodied voice that sounded in his head. It bewildered his already clouded mind. Was this just his imagination?

The voice told him not to despair. It told Antoine that he was a mind, not a body, and that he could overcome his situation within his mind. Was he on the edge of death? Was this the voice of an angel?

Antoine was as fragile as he was weak. He was hungry for food and thirsty for water. In desperation and despair, clinging to hope he had no other choice; he was willing to risk trusting the voice. He asked the voice how he could understand what it meant to be "a mind and not a body." The voice spoke back saying:

"I will teach you."

It was as clear and as vivid as one could imagine; he distinctly heard the voice speak, but the words did not frighten him. From that point on, he listened and absorbed the lessons the voice gave him, and the concepts it taught him. Antoine finally had welcome support and guidance.

In the months following, pre-occupied with learning about his mind, he was finally hearing something he could understand and take to heart as he still does today. The voice was seemingly of a higher source. Even though he could vividly hear it, he never saw a body, yet he knew that the voice was real. It kept him from going insane. It told Antoine that later in his life he would meet another person who would also share and understand these communications:

"You will meet a woman with whom I will communicate, and who will write all that I pass on to her."

The voice told him to share with the world what he had learned when he was finally set free. He would know when to make public his experiences and the teachings of the voice.

In this tight little cave, locked away from the world, he had become comfortable, in a way. Not knowing what the terrorists would do next to keep him from rejoining the outside world, Antoine shared with the terrorists what he was learning from the voice.

You would think that the terrorists would want to keep him quiet, but they just laughed at him. You would also think that they might find the decency in their hearts to alter his accommodations. But they did not care about his comfort; they simply assumed he was going crazy.

"Twisted terrorists," he thought. They did nothing to improve Antoine's living conditions; nevertheless, he persevered and did not stop talking to the terrorists about his newfound understanding. In this respect, the terrorists were no different from anyone else, Antoine thought. He knew that if you believed in something strongly enough, and you talked about it, someone would at least appreciate your reverence. He did not expect much more than that.

Eventually, Antoine's stories of his reliance on the voice began to have an impact on the terrorists. It captivated them. They were staggered at how he could live in such a minuscule space as this cave, endure the dreadful pain, and still remain so confident in what he thought was real. Antoine thought, "If you think you are a body, you can die. If you know you are a mind, you control the body. When the terrorists pulled the nails from my fingers, I firmly denied the pain. I did not accept anything of what they were doing, and I told the terrorists that if they truly knew what they were doing, they would certainly not do it."

The terrorists were dumbfounded with Antoine's convictions. He had developed an optimistic view of things despite the torture. He had become very positive despite having every reason to completely give up on his life.

In Lebanon, the sacred text of Islam is the Qur'an, divided into one hundred and fourteen chapters or suras, revered as the word of the creator, and dictated to Muhammad. The Qur'an is accepted as the foundation of Islamic law, culture, religion and politics.

Antoine knew that terrorists did not have access to any other book on religion other than their own. However, Antoine also knew that curiosity is a universal human trait. Relying on this knowledge about human nature, Antoine hoped that they would listen to him speak about the 'voice', the belief of any other religion notwithstanding.

Taking the risk of receiving increased torture, and taking the risk that he might offend the terrorists, he asked for a Holy Bible. He never thought twice that he could actually get something so remote from the region. And of course, being perceived as disrespectful could have angered them, especially with the thought of the blasphemous stories within this book. Perhaps the terrorists would pummel him just for the thought. Secretly though, they might have actually read the book themselves, afraid to tell anyone else. In time they surprised Antoine, not with a beating, but with the Holy Bible he had requested. Miracles can happen.

Antoine never knew what would come the next day. He no longer really thought of the past or future at all. He now lived in the present and never wondered about the next day because time was no longer his focus. "Tomorrow is today's future, and it does not exist today; tomorrow is only present when tomorrow becomes today," the voice told him. He now thought only in the present tense.

This is where things began to change course. Someone had ordered the terrorists to release him, unscathed further, to deliver him somewhere safe, to return him home. Antoine's faith in the voice must have caused gravity to unleash the terrorists' hearts. He would soon be free.

When he was told, he thanked them, but replied that he was already free for the voice had already shown him freedom.

Antoine never doubted his freedom was reality. His faith was strong; he knew that in the mind he was protected. He never challenged his learning. His testimony still is, that the voice is real and that we are all equally empowered.

Still, despite the wonderful news, there was something not quite the way it should have been. Apparently, his captors did not really want him to be free and still felt he should die. They never really believed he was anything but delirious from their beatings, and soon afterward, the torture began anew.

They picked up leather whips, covered his eyes, and began beating the bottoms of his feet until they bled. For increased pain, they would sometimes put his feet into freezing cold water after beating them, and then start the whole process over again. Repeatedly they would do this, only stopping when they became tired. Despite their orders to release him, they were not finished with Antoine.

Sometimes they tightly wrapped fishing line around Antoine's private parts, attached weights on the other end of the line, then hurled the weights across the room. Antoine's private parts would be painfully jerked upward in the knotted line, his body still cramped in the tiny cave. But Antoine remained silent.

Terrorism is harsh and brutal, inflicted on anything and anyone by individuals that believe they have the right to hurt, kill and destroy.

These unrelenting, hate-driven men sometimes focused bright lights into Antoine's eyes for lengthy periods, hoping this would blind him. His eyes were forced to remain open and the heat from the light dried out their fluids. Yet, though the light would be blinding to most anyone who had endured this unspeakable treatment, today he is not blind.

It is possible that the terrorists felt skeptical that Antoine could even exist as a functional human being at all any more. After a while, when nothing took his life, they began to wonder; they had inflicted a human being's body with horrific pain and suffering, and yet this human being did not faint or cry out.

Although the terrorists were more than a little hesitant to follow their original orders, they were finally forced to do so and eventually released him. For whatever their superior's "raison d'être", their faith or guilt was tested. Antoine's faith was tested as well.

The terrorists were persistent, but they had been stunned beyond anything they could ever imagine by Antoine's confidence. Finally, his ordeal had ended, and the pain was now over. This episode of Antoine's life had now become a memory.

Chapter Two

Over twenty years passed before Antoine would meet the person about whom the voice had spoken. Her name is Liliana, a young woman from Colombia. They are experiencing growth just as thunder announces the coming of a storm. This sequence of events tells their stories as disclosed by the voice of a being they have never seen.

It is rare to find a person that understands the basic laws of our inner nature as well as the academic disciplines of sociology, psychology, and the mathematics of our universe. Perhaps it is because this knowledge requires us to comprehend the history of the human race. Without this knowledge of the stories and studies that have preceded us, we cannot conjure up a complete picture of humanity's journey.

Only a few humble scholars have even come close, while experiencing the consequences of being perceived as insane, convincing no one, in the end, that they have found the truth. However, if you believe in miracles, anything is possible. Is it possible that Antoine and Liliana, because of having the courage and vulnerability to open their minds, were able to hear the voice and let it illuminate their way today, just as it did for Antoine when he emerged from the darkness of the cave that could easily have served as his tomb?

Antoine and Liliana do not offer scientific findings. They are not philosophers like Descartes. Nor are they mathematicians, scientists or even writers, just average people. They are as normal as the family next-door, but something extraordinary happened to them. The same could have happened to anyone, and we know that what Antoine experienced is not completely unique. Perhaps it is the fear of being considered crazy, opportunistic, or religiously fanatical that keeps many of us from speaking openly on the subject of spirituality. We are now witnessing the sharing of a series of exceptional events, a fascinating story of two people experiencing life at an unusually high level of spiritual awareness.

A sage said long ago that when we read with an open mind, we tend to learn, and when we trust our inner selves, we tend to make good decisions.

Once Antoine met Liliana, it was love at first sight; they were friends from the start. As a rule, we often do not bond quickly. We often guard our feelings from one another to lower the chances of being hurt. We take our time, study each other, and yet, there are still no guarantees.

The usual rule of experiencing a slow bonding process did not apply to Antoine and Liliana. Companionship and adoration can be a bond that can last forever, and it may be true that opposites attract. Antoine was a family man with children; he struggled to get his life going and successfully achieved an upscale lifestyle. Liliana was a model and an actor traveling in Hollywood circles. Single, in pursuit of the actors dream, she struggled too, but her struggle seemed more fun. After listening to the voice though, the fact that she and Antoine were opposites might have had nothing to do with their meeting at all.

Prior to Liliana and Antoine meeting, Liliana was immersed in her career. She was as confused and as busy as thousands of others in the Hollywood Scene, mired in a 'catch 22' lifestyle common to those "needing an agent to get a job, and needing a job to get an agent." The fast lane was the path she traveled.

She was an anxious individual. Her anxiety was fed trying to maintain her competitive edge over her fellow models, actors and agents. She did not know where the next job was coming from or where she would live next. Liliana was a typical young woman who took care of her physical appearance, as that seemed to be her meal ticket in this competitive business. She was smart, defensive, shy, and a loner.

She could not predict what was going to happen tomorrow. In this environment, she knew that it was essential to overcome her indecisiveness and to develop a positive attitude about herself in order to succeed. Each day was very much like the last. The drill was always the same, but not this particular day. As she sat looking out her window, sipping a cup of tea, she heard a voice that seemed to be coming from within her. Needless to say, it scared the daylights out of her. It was as real a voice as one could ever imagine. It spoke deliberately saying just a few words:

"You are a spirit."

It was mesmeric. The voice was vivid and all too clear, and it unsettled her. One can only imagine hearing it, seemingly coming out of nowhere. To Liliana this was not "cool". She thought she might be going mad. She focused all her senses and tried to move on from that unnerving moment. She did not understand how this could even be happening or even whom to tell. Perhaps it was the anticipation of her hectic schedule that morning that had her wound up in an emotional knot. She decided to take her usual run, and then the appointment she had to keep. Many in her line of work suffer extreme anxiety, desperately needing to get that next job. The imagination runs rampant with so much in the mind.

Liliana really did not want anyone to think she was losing her mind or that she could be hallucinating. Strangely though, she had a feeling that something positive was about to happen and that this would all make sense eventually. She did not know why, but somehow she felt optimistic.

How did Antoine and Liliana meet?

Antoine and Liliana met at an Academy Awards party in Hollywood. It was a chance encounter, but after that evening they were inseparable. They talked on the phone almost every day since Antoine lived in Newport Coast and Liliana lived in Los Angeles. During that time, they traveled the considerable distance many times to see each other. Their views and opinions seemed to overlap on all aspects of their lives, and in some mysterious way, things progressed very quickly.

They never questioned or even discussed what was happening to them. They knew in their hearts that being together was all that mattered.

It may not be possible to say what influences were at work, but the relationship quickly soared to the highest levels as a result of their transparency and honesty with each other.

After they started their new life together, for the most obvious reasons, Liliana did not tell Antoine she had heard the voice… not at first. She did not know if he would believe her. Furthermore, Antoine did not tell Liliana of his captivity nor of any of the teachings from the voice, at least not right away. He was still awaiting the sequence of events that the voice told him would come to pass. Nevertheless, he strongly sensed that she was "the woman" the voice had spoken about. As a result, with all of the quiet-time held between all three of them (the 'couple' and the 'voice') there was a stressful silence. Antoine felt that he was taking a risk by remaining silent, yet all three remained silent.

*****

After Liliana's first encounter with the voice, she had begun to awaken in the middle of the night feeling tranquil, composed, loved and protected. She felt compelled to write at the oddest times of the morning. She knew she would eventually need to tell Antoine.

One night when the voice reached Liliana, it woke her up out of a deep sleep and she felt an impulsive urge to start writing. It was as if she was experiencing a sort of domination, but she had no fear. She did not feel threatened.

The voice filled her with its presence, and when it spoke, it was like a bolt of lightning speaking from within her. She has now heard it many times, but nothing was as frightening as the first time. That night the voice instructed her to do something:

"Close your eyes to open your mind."

It was almost too much for Liliana to comprehend. As she summed it up in practical tone, "This is a voice I am still not able to see, I can only hear it, and it wants me to close my eyes while walking in the dark. That's it then. My mind will be open."

Had it not been for Liliana's faith and her strong wish to find harmony and love within her life, she may have not been curious enough or willing to listen. The voice certainly knew whom to touch.

The voice makes Liliana feel collected. She does not think of looking for the body of the voice anymore. It just feels natural. The voice speaks to them in English even though Antoine and Liliana speak English as their second language. As charming and as European as they may sound, neither has completely mastered the English language, but they certainly have a full comprehension of the voice.

Antoine may be fortunate, as he is not required to write. He communicates, listens and reasons with Liliana all the time on the subjects delivered to them.

Liliana is the communiqué. She writes what she hears from the voice that communicates with her nearly every night. She writes a full compilation of what she hears, many paragraphs that run sequentially. Everything she writes makes sense to her, and she is grateful that the voice has selected her to take down these words. Still, she is amazed by what she is learning.

Both Antoine and Liliana are convinced that their trust is compelling them to share a reality brought to them by the voice, and they are convinced that any person who reads these writings will learn from them.

"The voice, the spirit, the mind, they are part of us all. Antoine and I have chosen to listen to the voice the same way you, or anyone, can decide to listen. Our work is for those who want understanding and knowledge, and it all comes from the same source that is within every one of us."

By choosing the course they have taken, Antoine and Liliana are collecting a certain spiritual wisdom by listening to the voice's message and writing it down as they receive it.

A useful tool to attempt to understand the teachings of the voice is one that uses children as a metaphor: The normal two-year-old child does not have the ability to listen and understand everything that he hears. As the child grows and progresses through repetition and various forms of training, we can then understand the teaching method used by the voice. It can be fascinating to observe the progress. Through repetitive learning, Antoine learned courage while in captivity. Liliana gained wisdom, and by being vulnerable, learned how to trust. Seeing the result of listening to the messages, it resonates within us when we hear them again, whether in our memories or from the voice itself.

Both Antoine and Liliana express what they have learned and why this knowledge is so important to their everyday lives. The tools they offer may not always be useful for everyday living, but if you listen, you'll benefit. They are not writing a rendition of the events they are experiencing. They are communicating to us the words that come from a voice within them, and the voice wants them to relay all that they learn. Here then, the voice starts with the message to the world:

"The mind of creation is an extension of the complete mind of the creator. Equally, the creator and creation are ultimate powers.

Before time existed, creation decided to separate from the mind of the creator. After that, the mind of creation entered into darkness and fell into a dream-like state.

Having disconnected from love, knowledge, and everything it received from the creator, the mind-asleep was of limited power and became lonely. In its loneliness, solitude, and fear, the mind-asleep substituted the creator's mind with another mind; it made the ego-mind and forgot any memory of its real source, disappearing into darkness and self.

As a requisite for existence, the ego-mind required a promise that the mind-asleep would not remember its real source, and because it was lost, it agreed and let this be, vowing, 'I will.'

The ego-mind did not trust its maker; it was aware that at anytime the mind-asleep could change its mind. To prevent its maker from changing its mind, the ego-mind originated guilt.

After the ego-mind made guilt, a protection, it realized that the mind could not attack itself. Given that, the mind of creation is power, and the ego-mind can use this power within its own limitations, the mind made the body in conceptual time. Likewise, when the body is complete ...

- *It becomes a wall between the mind-asleep and the source; as our bodies' eyes are blind to the spirit, the spirit is blind to form.*

- *It projects fear and guilt onto itself and other bodies.*

- *Cause and effect reverses – (In reverse is when the ego-mind contradicts the laws of the source, and no longer the source is cause and creation is effect. The reality of the mind-asleep distorts and the mind will believe that the cause of its existence is in an external world.)*

- *The mind is embellished with the five senses (sight, hearing, smell, taste, and touch) and the body (or the world of form) appears as real.*

- *The mind considers the body real and consumes itself with worries and concerns for its physical needs, such as growth, health, surviving.*

- *The body and any form will go through evolution and death. Therefore, the world of time and form that is known as life is the world of illusions and death.*

- *The ego-mind / mind-asleep become everything that the mind of the creator and the mind of creation are not (death, sorrow, and form.)*

When creation fainted into a deep sleep, the creator knew that it would need a way to remember reality, which is creation's light. This sacred light is part of the mind-asleep, and when the mind becomes aware of it, it will awaken from its dream state."

See Illustration 1 on page 23: From the mind of the creator to the mind of creation, down to the separation line, is truth, reality and infinity; it is ageless and unchanging. Below the line of separation, the ego-mind (the self) and the mind-asleep are not reality. They are form and death in a world of illusion.

The three lines that join above the light-mind and the ego-mind represent consciousness, which is the mind after the separation. The mind acts and becomes a decision maker. This is free will, where the mind chooses between its reality and its dreams. Either the light-mind or the ego-mind will control the brain since the brain is part of the body, and the body is impartial.

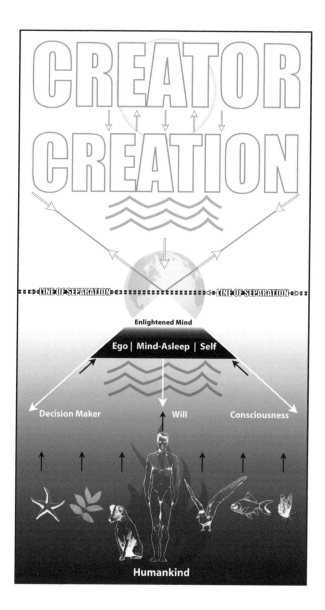

CREATOR

CREATION

LINE OF SEPARATION   LINE OF SEPARATION

Enlightened Mind

Ego | Mind-Asleep | Self

Decision Maker   Will   Consciousness

Humankind

Chapter Three

This book is about our search for truth, the most dominant facet of our lifetime. It came with a purpose that we may not have found had it not been for an unforeseen chain of events that overtook us. This is our testimony as we continue our search.

If it had not been for the power of creation, which was given from the creator, we would be in an infinite euphoria, all powerful with the creator. You would not be reading this literature as these words would not have been written.

Possibly, it was just having everything, like a child being served on a silver platter, which made creation yearn for more. Or was it simply having free will? These types of questions are open-ended and endless in regard to creation. In that case, it may be fruitless to ask what its reason was for separating from its source.

The voice taught Antoine and Liliana that energy is wasted when we dwell in the past. Rarely can we achieve anything of significance when we bar something from existing in the present. "The past has departed, and only now does reality exist."

Often we believe what we think is real when we conclude that what we see and feel is who we really are. When this happens, it is because we have allowed the ego and its form to blind us and to keep us from seeing true reality.

From the beginning of human consciousness, in one fashion or another, man has strived to understand his existence. We wonder what our bloodlines are. To date, the history of humankind is still not very clear on the subject. It is a study that will never end since we were endowed with a trait that has allowed the human race to survive. It is called curiosity. If the answer was as simple as saying "We are just one," then we could just be done with it.

Is there a definitive answer to the question why, if we view a creator as "love and life," we live on this earth in sorrow and regret? Could it be that it is because we think that we can love, and then turn around and take away the life that causes this conflict? How can anyone then claim he is carrying out the will of the real creator? The very structure of the human body is limited enough to endure pain, deceit, loss and death, hardly the work of a perfect entity. Perhaps, it is wiser to simply question what we believe and think.

"The voice knows our minds and we (Antoine and Liliana) know that the following text will raise questions. And, even though we have listened to the voice and are passing on its message, we are not interpreting what we are delivering to you. We are simply repeating. The will of the voice has chosen for us to tell everything that we learn from its words."

"In the world of which you think is reality, everything seems like a labyrinth that wherever you turn, you find a wall of what you have already seen before. You keep turning and you find no door or no window with the answer to the ultimate truth. That is because wherever you turn, you see nothing, since where you turn is in your mind, and the mind in which you choose to turn is the mind-asleep."

While this literature holds that the creator recognizes creation, as a parent regards an offspring, the creator is aware that his creation has drifted into other thoughts and does not remember him while sleeping.

Now, when observing an infant asleep, watching the innocence and delicateness of his body, we cannot see into his dreams. Nightmares may cause him to scream or have outbursts and tears. Or, if he smiles or coos in his sleep, we believe he is playing with angels. No matter what we observe, we do not know what the infant is dreaming.

Likewise, the creator knows when creation sleeps, but cannot know what creation dreams, only that creation is as pure as it is. This child is as innocent as the natural world that resonates the creation of the most innocent dreams. Like your dreams or the infant's dreams, they seem real.

Waking that infant while he dreams could cause him to experience discomfort. The creator would never wake creation, because it knows creation's will is its own extension.

When we wake up from sleeping, we know that our dreams are not real. When creation wakes, it is similarly fascinated and positive that it was dreaming and will inevitably remember what *is* real.

The creator is real and true. Truth does not change; it is what it is. An inspiration comes from a thought and thoughts can only come from the mind. Thoughts that change and contradict truth are unreal, for truth will not contradict itself.

If we believe that love sustains the world, it renders hope and the strength to move forward infinitely. Hence, the creator is love, and love is unconditional and supreme. Therefore, form within the realm of love is superfluous, lending less credence to love.

"When you think of love as feelings, it is not real. Feelings are sensations stimulated by the body and the body contradicts the truth in your mind. The truth in your mind is from the creator and love is in the mind. The mind is infinite and what is infinite does not end."

Just the same, the creator is the source of life, it is the reason we live. As a result, what is truly alive can never die. Think of the child afraid to sleep in the dark who asks us to leave a light on while he sleeps. In the same way, the creator left a light on in the sleeping mind of creation. That light is within our mind. It is hidden for our safety, but easy to find when we decide to recognize it. Open up to what you are reading, and if it makes good sense, it is yours to keep.

"Nothing that is real changes, and what you think you hold real, is what you believe. Knowledge is acquired; and once attained, it stays in the mind forever, even if it is hard to remember.

Knowledge can never be lost because it is part of the mind, and the mind is not form. Knowledge from the creator is not gone. It hides when the mind is lost with other thoughts.

A thought never changes. What seems to change is just another thought that opposes the first thought or agrees with it. Therefore, if the thought of the creator cannot be changed, in the least, the very opposite of a thought of the creator is what humankind has to question."

The ego is a mind. In our world, ego is an independent part of our character, which is, for the most part, arrogant and self-centered.

Reiterating that the ego is a mind, made by the mind-asleep of creation, it is a substitute parent in essence, where the mind hoped it would not face its fears. It would be like the person who has little friends that he talks to, that no one can see except the person that produces them. The ego then, is a mind in darkness, in fear and confusion.

Remember the child that screams in the middle of the night? The nightmares and the crying alone suggest the games or tricks played on the child. The ego controls the mind with fear. It will not stop unless the mind wakes to reality, and releases its fears and guilt. The reality of the mind has not gone anywhere; the mind is manipulating itself. Even if the heart fails, or the kidneys shut down, the mind does not die. Only the body is unreal. Interesting, isn't it?

The mind is immeasurable, without a physical structure. It has no beginning, nor does it have an end. Creation is likewise beyond measure and has never been any different; it is an endless present tense. Within infinity, time does not exist.

Forgetting a thought is not possible. As the mind that we are, we think that we forget, but we can actually never forget. Always, we select to remember only what we want to remember.

"When the mind-asleep remembers its reality, that thought will replace its illusive thoughts.

You, who have been taught that the mind is in the brain and maintain your awareness in all the functions of the body, do not remember that you are creation, and as that, with the world, you are one mind. The mind-asleep has disintegrated in different thoughts and each thought has taken a form.

The creator, being spirit, knowledge, entirety and devotion, it cannot identify with death, hate, sorrow and form. Therefore, the creator knows that creation is capable of awakening and can remember its real source."

There is a larger spirit within all of us, and it is in the mind, that which is from the creator and is part of the knowledge that is of truth. While it guides us, the spirit knows what we are looking for, like an intuitive parent who knows what is best for the child.

"Everything that you do is in pursuit of your truth. Your willingness to remember truth comes from within you. No one can coerce you to remember your source. You have a light that waits. It listens and recognizes what you ask for, and you cannot want what is not of you.

A world of war, sorrow and sickness, you want no more. That is why you are searching to find something of true meaning and that is the truth. Ask the light within you to show you the way to the source of life, which is your truth."

Chapter Four

When you believe that you belong to a certain race, living in an industrialized country that you may think is collectively more intelligent than any third world country, you are deceiving yourself. You may be different for any number of reasons, whether you are a group of persons or just one person, but you do not have the real picture. You will die not knowing who you are if you do not understand this concept.

Some of us think we are of one race or another due to, for example, the color of our skins. If we really want tranquility on earth, which is probably not possible at all, we could start by trying a little harder to understand each other. But it is difficult. Just try hugging a duck some time and see how easy it is being one with a creature that is different from you.

"Humankind and creation are one. Creation, in its sleep chose to accept the guilt because it was in fear of remembering the creator.

It is in your uniqueness with the body that the ego made you diverse. In your first glance of a person, what you observe is his body, and what you judge of that body comes from your own mind.

Creation does not have need of judging anyone, for it is one in the image of its kin. The world that the ego made enforces division, and this keeps the world detached with dispersed thoughts that judge.

Whether superior or terrible, everyone labels every movement that everyone makes. Everyone structures an image of every person, but it is only what is desirable that you notice. Judgment is separation from others and from your own person. You judge to provide sense to your own world because you are in your ego and the ego needs to give sense to its own world.

The bodies and forms that you notice in the world are not of truth. Within each body is creation. It is complete, loved and is one with you.

My voice, spirit, the true self, are one. I know that you are seeking truth, and now I am sharing with you these words of truth.

For centuries, you have tried to find the truth that is in you, and the truth of the world. Instead, you have only found a sea of deception and history of war.

You, who are creation, deserve to find the truth – your truth. The dream of creation has been so vast that there is no question the world is lost.

When the mind made the body, it made anything from ants to stars; women to men, trees to rivers, sand, clouds and the sea. It made anything you can name and everything that you want. The mind disintegrated into every possible form. That is why nothing in the world of form is equal.

You see difference, and so you assume that is how 'life' is. Life is life. In life, there is no death. You have thought of the opposite, that for something to die it needs to be alive. What you think is living needs to die to show you that what you believe is life will die. This is the reason the world has been confused.

How can anyone find purpose in life knowing he is going to die?

Why is there so much misery and pain during your idyllic time of life, if at the end you will die?

Creation, you are not damned to a world of pain and affliction. Know your realism. Unite with the world in the mind and return home where your family awaits you with love. Save yourself from the heavy load of sorrow and sickness.

The world of form is the illusion of creation. Absolve your kin from their illusion. Refute their ego. Without your kin, how can the unity of creation be real?

Deliverance is unattained by punishing yourself or by punishing others. You will not gain deliverance by giving gifts to your place of adoration or by surrendering your assets, or your desires. Deliverance is within you. It is within the acceptance of truth, the memory of the source of life, and the thought of love.

The separation is a mistake. It is the blunder of opting for illusions; it is the error of choice, which requires correction.

When the mind chose the idea of separation, it fell to sleep and it has since been asleep. Now the mind must wake from the dream of the illusion of the body to find its true self. When the body is awakening, it is awakened by the morning sun. For the mind to wake from the dream, it has to be from the light within. It is your own decision to accept your light, and to let your mind wake.

It was your decision to turn away from the light of life. It was your decision to choose in a different way.

Why would a creator create its creation with limitations? It is not the creator who takes life from you; that which you believe you have. Your own ego-mind finds no more use of the body and chooses not to see through the eyes any longer.

As the ego-mind departs the body, it falls into the unknown. In the unknown, fear seizes the mind and it selects what is familiar amidst its experiences. By choosing what it remembers, the mind obtains another body. Once the mind takes another body, its thoughts immerse in the new body. Its awareness wants to discover the new body, like the baby that does not remember that it is a mind. Creation does not die. Its mind is misplaced in a dream.

You are everlastingly bliss and love. What you look for in everything that you do, it reigns within you. Those who pray to a deity and dispute from their own conviction that truth is somewhere not in them, they are still probing for the truth. Truth can only be in the love that is within you.

The creator is love and love is truth. The world that you presume is outside of you cannot bring you the peace that you look for, because there is no world outside of you. The apple does not satisfy the hunger, but the thought of it will."

See Illustration 4.

"The venture into the world of idols does not bring you closer to the truth. Trust not in form for everything in form is part of the dream.

Your kin's body is his own mind's dream. You are a spirit who lives in completion through infinity. You are powerful and nothing could ever defeat you unless you allow it to.

Nothing can hurt creation. Besides, it can only be hurt if it chooses to believe that anything of the dream can hurt it. How real could that pain be, if after all, dreams and illusions are not real?

The human race has long believed that the creator is to punish everyone for its sins. He does not know of punishment, and has nothing to punish.

The creator knows of no pain and sin. Why would he want creation to suffer in misery and in terror of death?

The creator did not make the disasters of the world, the ego-mind did. Neither did it send away Adam and Eve from the garden.

The forbidden tree is form, Adam and Eve are bodies, and the garden is form. What is of form is not of spirit, and what is not of spirit is not reality.

Adam and Eve is a story written by humankind. It is a story written to keep the mind in fear of acknowledging a higher source. The story of the original sin was made by the ego.

Do not accept as true that each person in a body is a sinner and that the creator will punish the world for the original sin."

We know that we do not use all of our senses, especially those that we are not aware of, or may have never known. But we are not alone, for there are angels that are our friends, and they follow us all the time.

The voice is not asking us to view Antoine and Liliana as angels, just to listen if you are inclined to do so. After all, we all dance to some drummer, but we can choose which one that is, and the choices are numerous. Liliana repeats the words in script as she receives them from the voice. A substantial number of words that seem incredible at first later prove to be undisputable.

We have believed so many things in our lives, and most that we believe has become difficult to manage. We are fortunate to know of a voice that says we do not need to have a cluttered mind that is constantly possessed with preoccupation and fear. We are still a mind and not a body that has yet to be expressed in all its complexities, by some mathematical equation. Besides, who really knows? Einstein knew perhaps. The man who invented the theory of relativity was not a fanatic, nor was he a relativist. He believed that absolute laws of the universe exist. If this is true then, he may have asked the question: "Will we all live forever?"

Chapter Five

"The love that you search for is within you. It is so close to you that it is hard to see."

That particular love is you. How many times has your grandmother told you that Doris Day had it right? Even when you *think* you will never find love, you will.

"You will find love the day that you are willing to see. You will see when you remember to see. Your mind has been asleep and you have believed what you see is who you are. You have therefore made a world where you are the master and commander. You have closed your eyes so tightly that you have forgotten to see.

You have believed in solitude, and sadly depended on sickness, sorrow, confusion and a body. You think that you are fragile before the world of different forms and frequent changes, and you have long deprived yourself of love. There is no need of any fears anymore. You are love and you are your own strength. That is what you must remember to see within yourself.

Your heart is your soul, your spirit. Love is of the heart, it is of the mind. It is not of the body. What is in form is limited and love is limitless. Love is you. You are love and by being love, you have all. All is having the totality of the creator, the completion of creation and the remembrance of your real self. All is your power.

The world you think is out there is in you. By being in you, and you being love, the world should be all love. If the world is not a world of love, then it is not your real world. A world that is not of love must be an illusion because love is your reality. Love is your natural state of being. You, who wherever you turn, see a world of suffering where everything in it has the cost of pain; you should question, why would a higher source give such world of suffering to its child? Why would a creator deprive its creation from the joy, the love and the peace of life?

You are the child of a higher source. You are the child whom a higher source loves. You and all your kin do not belong to the world of body and form because that world is not reality. The world of humankind is a world of time and death, and both are limitations. Your home is heaven and you are a supreme mind. That is your reality; the reality that you do not remember. How can you remember reality when you are in a world of illusion and believe that you are a body?

The world of the body is the world of perception. When there is perception, there is projection. False perception is what the ego-mind made and gave to you; to insure that you would not remember you are a mind and not to question your true source.

You see a world outside of you and you blame that world for everything that you feel. You make it the cause of pain and of all that you think you are. You make the world accountable for everything that happens to you so you think not of the responsibility that what you see and feel is in you and made by you.

If you remember that the world is in you, you will remember your power and by remembering your power, you remember your creator.

Your mind fears your power. Your reality is love. A higher source is knowledge and heaven is certainty. When you understand, you know, and there is no doubt in knowing.

When you realize that there is nothing in you but the realm of creation, you will be in everlasting peace of mind and joy. The world of illusion, sickness and suffering will vanish and death will touch you no more.

The ego-mind made the body to separate and to attack given that the mind alone cannot separate and cannot attack. The mind, being formless, can only join and that is something the ego does not want.

Oneness is of creation. When you are loyal to the body, you ignore creation."

Everything that we learn is from what we see, and what we see has already become the memory our body attributes to another form. A higher source has no form, and that is why we cannot see a higher source. Some people think that when the body dies, they will find a higher source. How can their mind find truth when it remains attached to its memories of body or form?

"The source of life does not judge its supreme child because its child is perfect. The doors at home are open for the child to return, sinless and innocent as it has always been. Only, the ego does not want you to return. It has made you believe in dreams and it has made you think that the world is guilty before the eyes of the creator.

The ego-mind made all the appealing views and the ostentations of what you think you see. However, you have deemed the source of life created the moving world and therefore consider yourself vulnerable to all the differences. Everything that you see has a mind just like you; like you, their minds do not belong to their form but in heaven with the creator. Heaven is in you as it is in everything in the world. What you look for in everything that you do is also in you.

44

An attack is a show of violence toward something or someone; then, everything humankind does is an attack against reality. Reality is not form, it is the spirit; the choice for form is an attack against truth.

When you see humankind, and you judge it for what it is, you attack a kin that is one with you. When you attack your kin, you also attack yourself. Overwhelmed by perception, you are not aware that everything you do is an attack, because your awareness is engaged in responding to the needs of the body, which is an attack on your true self.

It may be hard for you to comprehend the true meaning of attack in relation to the truth. You have learned that attack is just a violent act. If that would be so, what then would anger, depression, sorrow, envy and sickness be upon your own self. Accepting the body is accepting the illusion and accepting illusions is attacking the sacredness of the world and of you.

You are lost in a world that is not your world. You have not been able to find yourself out of that world because right now what you remember is the dream, and in dreams, there is no reality. That is why to find reality is such a controversy and mystery to the world.

The ego made the body to keep the mind occupied with other bodies, blinding the memory of the higher source. Look on everything that the body needs. Look on how much time you spend on having families, on *competing with others; on obtaining houses and cars and going to places.*

Think of the investments that you put on taking care of the body so it does not get old, so it does not lose its vigor and die like everything in the world of form. From the moment that you wake, even when you are asleep, you think of the body's needs. Humankind does not spend enough time thinking how to recognize the creator.

A higher source is not in a certain place nor is it found at first-land. The fact that it is in you might frighten you. For ages, humankind has believed that the source of life is outside the self, and that it could only join with the creator under certain conditions or by certain deeds. Your higher source is love and it is everything that you know that is good and loving.

Since the beginning of time, which the ego made, the world has told many "stories" about reality. Each of those stories has had a source and its own set of principles."

Some of those stories could be convictions of friends or family members. They can be discussions of whom to like and whom to hate, of races that are undesirable, of languages that are foreign or slang that is characterized racially. Most of these ideas are irrational, but we are so much a part of it that it is hard to explain when it began or when it will end.

How to bring this picture into focus is not clear since we cannot seem to untangle our intricate knot.

If the above explanation is still unclear, consider asking this question: If everyone in the world comes from the same source, why then are only some people (the hierarchy) able to reach a creator, or their source? How could there be so many differences when the higher source is "one" and total?

Chapter Six

"*Humankind makes promises about what it believes to be the truth; when in fact it cannot provide what it does not have to give. A promise is when you 'will' to give something of value. You have nothing of your own to give but the 'will' of a higher source, and the 'will' of a higher source is not for you to promise. Promises are of the dream.*

When you turned away from creation, the ego knew that you could turn back and remember. It then made you promise that you will not remember. You followed the promise because you thought you had broken the will of the source of life. It is in that promise that you believe you are a body.

Every time there is a promise, the mind chooses not to be with the higher source because it is repeating the promise that it made against its truth. When you promise, you accept that illusions are real and you enforce the position that you are not in your reality. Hence, deep in your heart you know what you see is not real but you need to make yourself believe that it is real. That is why you promise and ask for promises.

Promises convince the mind that something is real when it thinks it is not real. When you make someone a promise, you enforce the separation given that your awareness is not in the truth. You separate from that person by setting his words not in accordance with your thoughts. You make him promise in order to have an agreement with him.

When you look at a man, what you are looking at is yourself. If you do not believe his words, it is because you do not believe in yourself. You have said that men have broken many promises and that they have not delivered their word, and that is why you do not believe whom anyone truly is. Promises are broken because when you ask for a promise, you mean for the promise to be broken.

Humankind must promise to prove it is right. In the ego, you need to prove yourself right. You need to believe in yourself and you need to believe that you can deliver your word.

If you speak with your heart to people's hearts, you communicate with truth. Therefore, you need neither something to prove nor a promise to hold, because in your heart, you know they are akin to you.

The language of the heart says all and gives all. Nevertheless, it is with your heart that you stop communicating when you judge an external world. When you judge a person as a stranger to you, you place the cause outside of you. By accepting his 'id', you will only hear what his ego speaks.

You want to believe in everything that everyone says to you, but in your heart you cannot believe in what they say because of all the uncertainties that you have been told. The world is a stream of promises that are gone, even though there is always the hope that something, somewhere, is to be trustworthy.

It is to your kin that I ask you to speak and listen. Speak to the supreme mind in them and they will respond only with truth. Speak to humankind's 'id' and you will get a tree of broken promises.

There was only one promise to be, the will of the source of life. You thought you could break that promise but nothing of a higher source can be broken. A higher source cannot break itself. In reality, the higher source and you are one; the same heart, the same mind.

A higher source has never left you. It is you, when your awareness is in the body, who thinks you are apart from creation. Your awareness cannot split in two. If your awareness is in the body, in all its senses, everything in the world of form will arise as real to you. However, if you withdraw your awareness from the body, you are in reality and you will not dwell in ideas of sin anymore. With the mindfulness on the senses, you cannot be yourself, for the *body is full with many things to keep you from remembering your source.*

The ego has made you think that the creator made the wonders of the world. It has made you believe that the higher source has given you the exciting moments of your existence that you treasure and that later are snatched away by the hands of sorrow.

The world you see is the world you accept.

The incessant feelings in your body make you rely profoundly on them. Every feeling is the awareness of the senses when stimulated. In addition, since every sense is always stimulated, you are at all times affected by the senses of the body. Everything that is and that happens in the world affects you. Good or bad, the mind is never at peace since any emotion is a disturbance of your peace of mind.

The ego-mind gives comfortable emotions. You believe in them; you think they mean happiness and joy, and you confuse them with peace. The ego lets you play with the idea of peace, but at any moment, it brings a thought or an event to disrupt your peace. Peace is complete and balanced.

You make a world in your mind of what is acceptable to you and what is not. You defend your world and your positions with pride and honor, but that world, at the end, will turn against you. The world in which you have put all your trust will disappoint you. You think that your source of life is the cause of misery. When you know you are a mind of spirit with no end, you will understand that the world of form and its misery is a dream and that nothing of what happens in it, even death, is part of you and the world's reality."

Gunner is a handsome, fluffy Persian cat. He sits next to Liliana when she writes and he purrs when he lazes on Antoine's chest. He is always where they are. His little ears perk up when Liliana reads, as if he understands what is said – perhaps he does; after all, he is a mind as well.

On one day of heavy work, with papers all over the desk, the computer on and the phone off the hook, Gunner persisted on being part of the whole experience. He refuses to stay down, so in a moment of impatience, Gunner is unceremoniously thrown out of the room. Once the work is finished, Gunner comes back to them with all his tenderness and love.

Antoine: "This world should learn from cats. They have a forgiving mind. No matter what we do, or don't do to them, they just keep giving love."

Liliana: "Hummm…you are right."

"You dream within the dream, and you dream within those dreams. First, when the body sleeps, you dream of fairy tales and flying fish. You dream as vast as the mind is. When you awake within the dream, you think what you see seems real because you have just been dreaming.

The other dream is the wakened body dream. What you see, what you touch, and where you are, is just a dream. However, since you are in the mind of insufficiency, you are still lacking with what you have, so you dream of what you do not have.

Wherever you look, you are in a dream state of mind, and all that you look for is in your state of mind. I say state of mind because you are a mind. Nothing is either outside of you, in a body, nor in any form. Your mind is in a dream of shadows, forms, feelings, emotions and thoughts. When it wakes from the dream, you will realize that the sick bodies, the brick walls, the lonely hearts or anything in the world of form, was just a dream.

When you wake, you will know that waking is the truth in you. As your mind decides to wake from the dream, the ego will go along with your ideas, and it will make you feel any kind of feelings for you to think you have wakened to reality. However, at any given moment, the ego will bring you back to its control by stimulating the sensations of emotions.

Feelings and emotions are part of the body, and what needs to wake is the mind. You are to wake to the reality of your mind. What you have in the mind is memories and what you experience is based on those memories. Only from memories can you judge. For you to not judge, you need the light of your spirit to dispel the memories of the dream for the truth to shine within you.

Stop for a second, ask yourself who are you and where do you come from. If you are the child of the creator, and I know that you are, is not the child just as the creator? Then, if you are not the child of a higher source, of the creator, who are you then? Think, neither in the future nor in the past.

Think in present, in this moment, and let your heart answer your thoughts.

What you hear from your heart you cannot contradict. There is nothing to contradict, for how can you contradict yourself? Only in the dream, the mind contradicts because it has to defend its own confusion. In your reality, you have nothing to defend for you are certain of yourself. Truth is in your heart, but if you insist that the body is your truth, you then contradict truth.

A higher source will not compel its child to wake, knowing that its child has the will to remember his truth. However if the awareness of the child is still in dreams, it may be because he wants to sleep longer and continue to believe in his dreams.

The ego-mind can fool you, but your heart cannot. It is in your heart where you have to look to find what you are lacking, and what you wish to find. However, it is in your heart where you do not look. You look at yourself in the mirror and you judge the world from what you see in yourself on the mirror, which is not the heart.

When you close your eyes, you can see how far you can go. In your mind, you can go far and be completely free. You can travel in time and do whatever you want to do. Imagine how it will be, if you turn from the ego and go to the supreme mind where you recognize the source of life. The limited mind cannot let you imagine that far. In that same way, a higher source cannot imagine the limitations of its child's dream."

The limited mind cannot see the infinite mind. Imagine having all and being completely free of fear and sickness. The mind is free when liberated from limitations. When you accept that you have a supreme mind and you become one with your own mind, you can have the certainty that everything in the dream will be provided, if you really want it.

"You have the power to choose anything. Everything that you want you will get. The mind-asleep does not know how to ask because it only has an idea of what it thinks it wants. What humankind wants is not what it really wants. Everything that the 'id' desires is to sabotage the peace within and to distract the mind from the realm of creation. Your spirit gives you what is in your heart; it is the only one in the world who understands your mind and knows what it really wants.

Your 'id' is dragged by a so-called destiny. Destiny is the rope that the ego has tightened around your arms. Destiny is nothing but the condemnation in you. Of destiny, you say that where you are, and what you are to be, is in the messages of your birth. You then wash all the responsibilities off your hands and say, 'the poor are bound to be poor and the rich to be rich.' The higher source is always fair with its children. In the dream, the mind chooses to taste the hunger of the poor or taste the anxieties of the rich. Destiny is of the future and the future is a prolongation of the past. Since the past is not real then the future is the same, not real. Destiny is not real. It is simply a false impression."

<u>Chapter Seven</u>

It is two in the morning, sometimes it can be twelve or one; these are the hours that the voice awakens Liliana. At times, the voice starts with a sentence right away and she has to hurry to her notebook. Other times, the voice calls her, "child, child" until she awakens and responds. Her tiny lamp barely lights the notebook where she writes down what the voice is telling her. She writes so fast that sometimes it is hard to understand her own writing.

She writes for several hours without ever moving. Once the voice stops, she heads back to her bed. In the morning, Liliana reads to Antoine what she wrote. She wonders how people will understand such concepts. Antoine says that during his time as a hostage, the voice gave him visual pictures for his understanding. Those images are the illustrations contained in this book, and have been created to help us open our minds to a better understanding of what we may see as non-related concepts.

"Nothingness is of the dream: a higher source is all. What the dream seems to provide is from its nothingness, and what turns to nothing has come from

nothing, including your body. Only you make the body real to yourself because it is you who gives meaning to its existence. Once the body is gone, what you have given meaning to will be there no more. During your existence, what you or anyone does in the body or with the body is without true substance since it follows the mind-asleep, and that mind is false.

Before the separation, there was no right or wrong, there was only the spirit. It was after the separation that the mind fell asleep. Therefore, the mind-asleep is a dream. Whatever comes from the mind-asleep, whether it seems to be good or bad, it is not reality.

If you feel persuaded to hurt another, then you do not believe in reality. The body that you think you can hurt is an illusion of your kin. Life is not of the body, it is of the mind. It cannot be of the mind-asleep, because it uses the body to die. Life is of a supreme mind, which lives infinitely and never dies. Therefore, humanity needs to think like the supreme mind to remember its source. Release your mind from the dream and the actions from the body will represent love. To release the mind is to change perception. In doing this you will see the world, not with vengeance or judgment but with love.

The world believes no one is supreme. In truth, what comes from the body is truly insignificant. A kiss, a caress does not have meaning at all, unless it is accomplished with the supreme mind. Yet still, the meaning will only be in the mind, not in the action. The bite of a fruit can be the same as an act of love when you are in the supreme mind; it transmits the supremacy of love.

You have the ego-mind, which is of no truth, and you have the supreme mind that conveys reality. It is your choice.

When you are in the ego-mind, nothing that you do is an act of love because the ego knows of no love. When you are in the supreme mind, everything that you do will be an act of love since all will have the same meaning, love.

They are two different minds. One is the mind of love and the other is the illusion of love. The ego is just an illusion, and the more you turn to the ego, the more you empower its illusion. You can only be in one or the other.

If you want to change because you want certainties and you want truth, let your spirit guide you through the dream. Your spirit is the one that corrects the mind from its forgetfulness. It permits the remembrance of your reality. Through your spirit, you find the supremacy of the world and you can return to creation where you will find all that a higher source has given you.

Humankind has experienced many "acts of love" and "charity". It supposes that if it does something good, that good and goodness will be returned. Goodness cannot come from the world. Goodness only comes from a higher *source. The ego just wants to give the illusions of goodness in order to mimic truth. It tries to mimic truth, but what comes from a higher source is shared with all and is infinite. If you want to do well, all you have to do is to share your heart with the world.*

Sympathy for a sick man and mourning a person's death is part of the imagining of doing well. It is not truthful because you are condemning that kin to his ego, and ego is death. You have the power to illuminate the world with love. Love fills all the world's needs. If you ask your spirit, its light will illuminate every man's mind. The light dispels his chosen thoughts of misery, anger, depression and judgment. Ask your spirit to shine on you as well; what you see from the world of form is in you and you need it to be released from your mind.

When you are with your spirit, you become one truth with all. The whole world is supreme and there can be no disparity to hold any criticism."

The mind of the child of a higher source of the murderer in the jail is as supreme as the mind of the child of a higher source of your dearest friend. If we do not see them like that, then we are saying that we are better than a creator is. How would a higher source judge its children but as itself?

"If you want to be free, lay judgment aside, see the beggar and the leading man the same as you see yourself in your supreme mind. Nothing brings you freedom as surely as the release of judgment. With that release, the mind is free.

You classify everything in the world, you give meaning to everything and you lay claim to what is valuable to you. It is like having your own train and entourage. The passengers that you value the most are at the front, and the ones you care for the least are in the back. Everything in the world, from parents to kids, spouse, friends, your boss, even the houses and the cars and the degrees that you hold, are baggage in the train. Everyone in the world has their own train that rides with them, except each one sits with their entourage differently.

All this diversity comes from the world of differences. You think the people in your train are better than other people in other trains and that they should be loved and treated differently.

Humanity's actions are rooted on fear. Since you are in a body, which is not who you truly are, you are in danger of being judged, therefore you are on guard. However, who is really judging whom? No one compelled to judge but you. What you think you need to prove, you only need to prove to yourself. As humanity's actions are grounded in fear, they are also full of guilt because the body opposes reality and manifests itself in the projection of that guilt.

It is very difficult for men to see the world as they see themselves. It is difficult not to judge, for judgment is learned throughout existence. Think of seeing the whole world as part of you. The ego makes you believe it is impossible and it will make you think there is no such thing as making the whole world a part of you. Its cleverness will make you ask, 'How can it be that I am the same as the clergyman, the cripple, the tree, the cloud, and everything that is different in shape and form?'

The ego will not let you accept that you are of one mind with every person or thing that you see. If you join with the world, the mission is finished. The ego confuses you. It might let you entertain the idea of seeming one with a person. It might let you select the people you want close to you so it feels good to you. You may like to be one with a princess or a queen. However, when you see the illiterate, the ones you laugh at and the ones that you resent, you might not like it at all; the 'id' does not want to see itself as one with them.

If you unite with the world in the mind, it means that you are uniting with a creator. Your deliverance lies in how you see the world. You owe people your freedom in the same way that they owe you their freedom. Be thankful to them, as they will be thankful to you. For every moment and every opportunity they give to you, as you give to them, allows you to be free and enter through the doors of your heart. How badly do you want to be in the realm of a higher source? How much peace do you want? It is all in your hands.

The supreme child has the extension of his creator's power. If you know you posses that power, would you keep giving that power to an illusion? It is your power and it is your choice.

The ego will do anything to prevent you from remembering the truth. It will teach you the opposite way of everything. It will make you think: "I am a fake." "My voice is not real."

I communicate love and shine reality's light into the darkness of the mind. I want you to find what you long for. You are the child of a higher source and I want to help you find your deliverance from any pain you are enduring. I want to restore your truth.

You, who cry and think in terror of death, need to know that those tears have just been a dream. You have been lost, looking for the road, and now you have found it. Your spirit will guide you and ensure that you will not get lost again.

You already have all the peace that you want. See no past and hold no judgment. In infinity there is no time, therefore time will not be when you cease to be."

See Illustration 5.

"When you long to see a person in body or form, the ego wants to prove that distance and form are real. You do not need to long to see anyone in their body, for they are always with you. When you long, you enforce distance; and as you accept distance, you then desire closeness. The memory of your life is within you, and it is there for you to keep and or heal it. Every moment is a moment that requires healing. If you think that you have healed a memory, and it still comes back, you are choosing to keep that memory. If you are living in a memory, you are living in the past.

Time passes, and in timelessness you find truth.

What do I want and who will provide? Ask yourself that question. Respond with the assurance that the world can only give nothingness. Do you really want to live? Let your spirit guide and teach you the way through the dream. The dream is the world of not knowing; and you will remain lost in a body if you follow the guide that does not know.

The world of form is not your reality, yet, you cannot ignore it for it is from the world of illusions that you must heal. What you have started must continue until it is finished. The body is still there, where you are. It is designed to exist for a certain time, and during that time, it has needs to be fulfilled in order to function. However, you cannot make the body your reality. How can you make the body real when it is only temporary and when it will not last?

You cannot make what is <u>not real</u>, real to you. <u>What is real</u> will not be real to you and you will stay in a state of confusion.

Your own dream will continue until your body perishes. It is just a matter of how you want to exist. Do you want to pursue the dream in uncertainty and cry in misery because of the guilt that you carry on in the ego-mind? Or, do you want to be free and play in the dream with joy and total peace of mind? It all depends on which mind you accept as your reality."

Liliana's brother comes to visit her, perhaps to see her way of life on the West Coast. During lunch in a neighborhood restaurant, she shares her writings with him. He tells her that there is no such thing. He says God created life, the body, and that all is perfect. He bombards her with questions and objections. Liliana becomes very agitated. She has never been questioned in such a critical way. Since her first experience with the voice, she has accepted the teachings from the voice with absolute and devoted faith.

"Your spirit teaches you how to be free. It leads you to a higher source and when the body dies, the form of the dream will not matter. You will be with a higher source and you will be saved from pain and deceit in a new existence.

The creator that the world advocates is of the ego itself. The notion that you are to be punished will lead you to a sea of tears, and the ego will drown you with no hope of survival. With your spirit, you are in the mind of the source of life and you will end the dream free of the burden you have given to yourself. You will see what is to come and you will have what has already been given to you.

If you are in a state of fear, you are exposed to attacks, possibly beaten and hurt by others. You are powerless. With a higher source, you have the power of creation. By realizing the power of the mind, you will have the ability to use your mind to weather the unforeseen storms of life and overcome the chaos with the love within you. You will replace chaos with serenity. By embracing the power of your mind, you can dispel the madness of the world that rages around you. To wake from the dream means that the mind is no longer in fear; you know your supreme reality.

By waking to the concept of timelessness, you can free yourself from the needs and desires of the body. It is to see that nothing you thought you were is who you really are. The body will not go anywhere when you wake from the dream. The body will continue its functions of formation and disintegration but it will not depend on thoughts from the past; it will transfigure the light from the mind of love.

If you want to continue living in a fantasy world, at least understand that the world of form is not real and that the body in which your mind abides is not you. Understand that it is up to you to make the world of body real - or not. Know that your spirit's light shines in you forever as long as your mind is asleep.

The ego-mind will persist, arousing the body until you 'will' to let the ego go. It brings memories for you to feel, it puts you in circumstances for you to be hurt and feel pain. It turns on all the senses connected with your feelings to give the impression of not being in control. Its existence depends in your trust of the body. However, with the love of the truth, the ego will transform to love by following your heart."

Chapter Eight

After her brother's departure back home, Liliana meets Antoine at a café on a cliff. They enjoy the golden light of the sunset and the delicate haze rising from the crashing waves. They have a smile on their faces as they contemplate the perfect view:

Liliana: "You are cherishing this."

Antoine: "Sometimes when I see this beauty I ask myself, how can this not be real? Then, it all hits me. But later I say, 'Why choose this limited existence in a body to suffer, work hard, get sick; and no matter how beautiful or good anything is, it will end or simply disappear?' It is like everything disappoints you."

Liliana: "That sounds negative."

Antoine: "Not when you release the idea that everything is outside of you and you join with all in the thoughts of love."

"When it comes to love, the ego is very clever. It knows how to deceive and make believe that you truly love something or someone. It tries to elevate you to a higher

state, but later, the feelings of love disappear. Those feelings emerge as real, and you trust they are of the heart, which seems to you to be of the heart; but really, they are of the body.

In the body, humans love in response to visual stimulus; they feel the sensation of "liking" the other body in their body. Love of the heart is a union and not at all temporary. How can what you feel be of the heart when you see yourself as a body and not as one heart and mind with all? These sensations of the body that you call love are illusions of love because you are still in a dream state.

Humankind confuses love with the attraction of the body. When you first join with a person in the mind and together share love with each other and to the world, be sure that the body responds towards each other with love. When you love in the heart, you love unconditionally. The mind of love is free of conditions.

In the dream, when you give, it is possible to win or to lose. If a boy gives a flower to a girl, she takes it and he has the flower no more. The girl might give him a smile and so that he has gained from what he gave. Humanity assumes that when it gives it will receive something in return. In the world of perception, that is the general rule. In the world of the mind, when you give, you gain and keep what you gave, because who you are giving it to is in your mind and your mind is you.

Giving and receiving is the mechanism of humankind. Giving and sharing is the mechanism of the mind. That is why, if you give to please the body, you might not get the love that you expect. Whereas with the mind, the more you share the love within you, the more it grows in you. The more you share the peace and the joy of a higher source with the world, the more it grows in you. What you give and what you share, you keep, and you cannot give what you do not have.

The laws of action and reaction are of the body since perception is part of this law. The mind sees itself apart and gives different meanings to what it sees.

You spend all your time thinking thoughts. Think now of what my words ask you. What do you value? What do you have? What do you want to give? You can only give what you have and you only have what you value.

Only by thinking can you answer since you are a mind of thought. The answers to those questions tell you who you are. Who you are determines what you want. Ask' yourself who you are. All that heaven wants is for you to find yourself. You cannot depend on anyone or anything to find what you want. The reason why you cannot depend on anyone else is because you are free to know and to choose for yourself. No one can influence your mind. No one can force you to think what you do not want.

Thinking is effortless, and the way to correct your mind is by changing your thoughts. To think requires neither special strength nor effort. You just need willingness to want to correct and to think for yourself. You need to find the will to turn to your spirit who helps you make corrections. If you do not want to correct your mind, then you have chosen to dwell in the mind of darkness. You then prefer to be condemned to the body that suffers in misery rather than to find your truth. Remember, you will choose what you ultimately want by knowing what you like to keep."

After a series of delays to meet her friend, Liliana finally makes her way to Los Angeles. She was as excited as when she was to tell her brother. Liliana shares her inner thoughts with her friend. But as she begins to talk, she notices that her friend avoids looking into her eyes. Liliana tells her that she is going to renounce her ego and to detach from the world to achieve peace of mind. Her friend tells her, "You are crazy. I love my ego and I don't care." She gets up and leaves.

"When my voice conveys not to give more value to one particular body, what it means to say is that when you have exceptional feelings toward someone, you think that person is better than another. Therefore, from the whole

world, you separate yourself from others and you make separation special.

If you separate from everything and give value to what you separate, you mean the world of loss is better than the source of life. If you are one with everything then you are with reality, and in your mind you love all the same.

It is with your mind that you love all the same so if you are still thinking on the body level you will confuse love with lust. To love everyone the same is the most difficult thing for humankind to comprehend; it does not mean that you are to share the illusions of every person. Each body forms a pure spirit, and it is for you to share in the mind the love that is within you. If you make someone or something special, you weaken your power; and power is not of the ego no matter how forceful its demands are.

Even with the breeze that caresses the skin, you have a special relationship, given that you see it as separate from you and you use it for your own pleasure or physical needs. What you make special is that one thing that you want selfishly since the 'id' never sees what it really is, but what it wants it to be.

A special relationship is selfish and destructive. It is selfish because it is only special for what it gives to you. Its destructiveness lies on the conditions that you give to the relationship. You give what you want but you also demand what you want. You satisfy the other's needs but with the condition that they satisfy yours. In addition, when there is nothing more to satisfy, the exceptional is not special anymore. It means that you are lacking love because you are not yourself and you want to be complete.

You think that you are to be complete with what is keeping you incomplete. In the dream, you would never be complete regardless of how unique the world makes you think you are to other people; and how significant certain people are to you. The ego's mission is to keep you in fear and to puzzle you with the idea that its world will complete you. You will remain seeking for completion until you realize and accept that nothing from the world of the ego can make you whole, even the special feelings that you hold towards those you seem to love.

There is an abundance of special relationships in the world and each one has its own terms to meet. Men and women bring their conditions to every relationship based on what they learned from the past and on what they have experienced. As the relationship goes along, more conditions are added since the terms that were met before did not satisfy them at all. You, on the other hand, also have to reply to a list of conditions. This is why relationships only last as long as the conditions are satisfied.

Special relationships are not of sharing but of giving and receiving. The exception of every relationship is its terms. They are significant to you because of how much you will receive at the end.

When you individualize with exception, you are in the ego and not with creation, which means that what matters to you is what you receive in the relationship and what satisfies your desires.

* * * * *

If you say that a higher source is everything, it means that its children are nothing. The creator cannot be without creation. If a higher source is special, then its children are not, and if its children are not special then a higher source is not. Therefore, you deceive yourself. The source of life has no conditions for you. You are its child and you are one with it and with creation. Would the creator put a condition upon itself? No. Conditions are of the ego.

There is no need in making a higher source exceptional because it does not make you exceptional. If the creator makes your kin exceptional, what would you be to the source? Nothing; you would be deprived from its love. You have to love the world equal with your heart.

Special relationships are not of love, they are fear. Every moment you are with someone or something, and you do not join in truth, you make it special. Even the bread that you eat at dinner will be a special relationship to you since the bread is satisfying the hunger of the day. If you share the bread with a higher source, then it will become a part of everything. Therefore, instead of having a special relationship with the bread, it will be a union of love.

Special relationships are of pain, disappointments and limitations. When you enter into a unique relationship, you have expectations and even though you seem to receive what you want, you will not get what you ultimately expect. Special relationships are from the past, they replace what the past took, and they give what the past did not give.

In the present, there is no past and no conditions. You are whole and you do not need to give to receive. Whenever you see a person, release everything from the past so that you become one with him or her and the exception will be no more. If you still feel the need to be special, ask your spirit to restore your truth since the need to be special comes from the fear of the separation.

Humankind does not value you for who you are, that is why you do not want to be special to anyone in the world. How can the ego value you, if when you die it deserts you and replaces your body with another?

Humankind only sees what to get from you and how to gratify itself from you. If you are making something special, share it with a higher source. The conditions are then gone and the relationship transforms to be truthful and complete.

Why not take a step forward and let the world see you as you really are? Why would you want to remain limited by the conditions of the world of the ego? You can show the world your truth by sharing it with your mind. The world will see the perfect you, because the world is one.

Everything that you do defends your identity. If your identity is so important to you, why not restore your real identity? Identify with your true self and defend that identity from the dream. The world will never stop making itself real to you. However, why let something that is not real and knows nothing tell you who you are? Undo the individuality from the world and find the fulfillment knowing that nothing from the world of illusions can ever give.

Release the need for exceptions, for they are not part of your real identity. It is your 'id' that wants the special relationships; nevertheless, no relation is significant without the union of a higher source. When you are with a kin in sacredness, you raise reality. If you love a person, then free him or her from the conditions and exchange the terms for the true love that they deserve to remember.

Choose no past and ask your spirit to be with you, and make of that relationship and everything else that you do, a virtuous relationship. Your spirit will release you both from all conditions and it will bring the relationship into infinity.

The more you release illusions, the more you restore truth. You may think you lose a friend if you release the unique side of the egoistical relationship, but instead you will gain a kin that will be with you forever and always through infinity. Even to those to whom you resent, the grievance is the exception in the relationship. If you do not release the resentment, you will keep it with you and you will be bound to the misery of the ego. Free your kin from his ego and gain the purity of his soul that you share with him. Be in peace. It is the real relationship.

Since your birth, you have only related to personal relationships. As a child, you depended on the relationships with those who understood more than you do; and throughout your existence, you continue dependency on others. You become dependent on your dependency. Even upon the air you breathe, you depend.

You may say: "I need to breathe to live", since everything in the world you do is for you not to die. Therefore, what you need you use, and what you use, you need to receive. It is inevitable that you will do whatever you need to do not to die, even though it is just as inevitable that you will die anyway. There lies the fear of the ego that everyone uses to survive. However, you cannot survive from a body that is already dying.

How you use the body is a form of an attack that you cannot avoid unless you first deny the ego. Accept the child of a higher source of the world and join with them in the purity of reality. You must include everything around you.

You cannot stop drinking water to quench your thirst, nor wearing clothing to protect you from the cold. The dream functions in a way that you must continue until the body withers. You can be conscious on what you choose to see in the world. You can accept the real self of every person, or you can judge from the illusion that your mind has been bound to believe. Where you are is a dream and not reality."

A sailor had a very sturdy boat, but after a storm came and smashed the boat, the sailor went into the woods. With some pieces of wood, the sailor made a small boat and went happily back to the sea. This metaphor means, if the dream can provide good fortune, enjoy it with gratitude and generosity. Do not become attached to the struggles and to the pleasures that the dream appears to give. What you have materialized does not matter. What matters is what you love since what you love is who you are. Nothing of the world should be unique even if you think it is dear to you. Your world is not the world of reality. If you hold precious anything from the world of non-reality, you treasure death.

Chapter Nine

It was a cold night when Liliana got up to write. While she walked toward the room where she writes, she experienced a fear that was beyond comprehension. Liliana was not afraid of anything in particular but in spite of herself, she started trembling with fear. She wanted to run to another room and hide! She was paralyzed. She wanted to call Antoine but she could not even speak. She hid beneath the blankets and stayed there shivering and sweating until she fell to sleep.

"I have said not to make a higher source special because there are no exceptions in the realm of creation. All is one, and it is where your spirit resides. The world wants to believe in the design that it is susceptible to pain and death. If you believe in the ego, you identify with it. In opposition to the infinite, it controls you by shortening your existence.

The ego is insane for it is the source of hate and darkness, and it makes you suffer until it destroys you. However, nothing from the ego is real. So, why identify with something that is false, even insane?

The body is a form that ignores all that you know. It learns from the ego, which is heartless. If you want to know how confused and fiendish the ego is, I can tell that in your heart you already know. You know it because at the highest point of your most exciting moments, you know that there are others dying in misery.

When you are jubilant, you hide behind laughter. You have either experienced sorrow or seen it happen. The mind hides what it needs to hide to use its best interest. It keeps every memory of everything that the body sees or experiences to use later against you.

The mind brings out every memory that it has, one by one whenever it needs to for the body to attack itself and/or the world. The ego manipulates the body for its own interest. It makes the body perceive the world it wants; for the world that you see is only a reflection of your memories. The ego uses the body to hide the fear and the guilt that opposes love.

If you make a body special, you really have nothing special. If you say that it is not the body but the mind that you hold dear, then it is the mind that embraces a higher source. There is nothing special to hold in a body. A body has no function without a mind. Without the brain, the body cannot move, but the brain cannot function without orders from the mind. Therefore, what moves the body is the mind. Every action that you see of the world starts from the mind. Thought comes first and then the body reacts."

See illustration 3.

"That is why I, as spirit, come to you to reach out to the supreme mind that is in you. When you experience joy, you are experiencing goodness and love. Those thoughts that stimulate happiness are the remembrance of your own nature. However, do not underestimate the ego, for it is ingenious. It lets you have elated moments in the remembrance of pleasure and satisfaction; but you can be sure that the delight will not last. The ego does not let you taste all its vileness; otherwise, you should be repelled and seek a way out. The mind-asleep needs to imitate heaven; it needs to make itself believe that the world is a wonderful and a perfect place.

What is perfect is unchangeable; however, everything that has form is ultimately changeable. The ego needs to let you sip fine wine, get intoxicated, and therefore not taste the food. The food represents its evil intentions. Those moments of goodness and love are the illusions of truth. They become infinite when you find them within you.

Remember truth child; you have been in a dream all this time. That body that you thought a higher source created is just matter which the ego-mind made when you gave it power once you found yourself in fear of separating from creation. Truth is the same for all humankind. Do not make the dream special any more. Ask yourself, what has it given you?

Forget the moments of gratification; they are like the fine wine consumed at a feast. Your reality is that you are a sacred spirit. What you experience is a dream state that your mind accepts as true. Your spirit lives in infinity and it will convey the truth to your heart if you release all the illusions that distract you from opening up.

The ego may be opposed to what you hear; however, your heart will know when you have heard the truth.

You depend on your mind to guide you and to teach you. That is unfortunate if you choose to depend on the ego-mind. No matter how many good things it seems to give you, it will always lead you to your destruction. On the other hand, you have the mind of light and knowledge.

Decide and think, not with the 'id' but with your heart. Ask yourself, if you want to go to heaven or hell. Do you want to live or die? When you answer these questions, you are choosing your guide.

The ego will guide you to chaos. Your spirit will guide you to infinity. With the ego, you have to work hard, figure things out, lie, cheat and sacrifice. You pay a terrible price until it leads you to misery. With your spirit, you need do nothing. It loves you as a higher source loves, and it does all that you need in the dream for the dream to proceed with ease and happiness.

You, who are constantly tired and tired of doing things in order not to be tired, ask yourself those questions and select your guide. The ego is not easy to release. How can you leave it when you made it? It will resist letting you go. It needs your power for its own existence and it survives on the loyalty you put on it. Your dependency on the world is your attachment to your memories. It is from those memories that the ego feeds itself.

To think in the present is where you can find reality; and without thought of the next moment there is absolute peace. In every moment that you think of something you are going back in time, and this seems to make time real to you.

When you think of these words, they are memory; your world is a memory. What you see, what you think and what you feel, are all memories. You may think it is not, but it is, because humankind has the illusion that time is moving forward.

When the body hurts, when you feel depressed, sad, lonely, or anything that relates to the senses, understand that it has come from your thoughts; and you can choose to eliminate those feelings and those thoughts.

You experience how you want to feel for as long as you want to keep a thought. The ego will not let you find which thought is stimulating feelings. Needing to find the memory would be lingering in the past. If you do not like how you feel at any particular point, you can recognize that your mind is causing the pain and the emotional disturbance. Bring those thoughts to your spirit for it to shine its light.

You have given power to the mind that dwells in thoughts of anguish, and you can take that power away from that mind. You fear the power within you because you have accepted the scheme that you are powerless.

When you feel uncomfortable with anything regarding the body, your heart reminds you that your reality is a spirit. Sometimes you think that you are at ease with your decisions, but in fact, you just pretend to be. You need to pretend that you are yourself to believe that you are yourself. In addition, since the mind pretends the existence of the body, when you do what you like, you do it with some sort of built-in guilt. You cannot "see it" or "feel it," but the guilt has already been absorbed. The guilt is in the body and in the external world. It is in something that is not real. Only you make it real. Humans plan their existence when they are afraid to look within themselves.

As a mother bares a child, she is doing something against her innocent nature. When you use the world to satisfy your hunger and bodily needs, you are doing something against your supreme nature. When you feel pain, you know deeply that it is not from your reality. Yet, you still admit the pain of the world."

Liliana cannot stop thinking about everything that is now part of her life and how it all encompasses what she is learning. She has many questions and she knows whom to ask. There is no time and place for Antoine and Liliana to go over what she is learning, but by looking into his eyes, she knows when he can respond.

Liliana: "Since I should not make my mother special, can I still be as affectionate with her as I have always been?"

Antoine: "You do not have to treat her any differently. In this world, she has a title and you should have respect for her; but you should not own her as your mother. See her as a pure spirit and love her as you love all. Which one is stronger, to love and have all, or to just have pieces?"

"Looking for something that you could not get before leads to anticipation; you expect something that you know you cannot have. You have trusted the world of bodies and it has disappointed you. When you start feeling that you are not getting what you want, you change and disguise what you want. Where you believe you are is an

organization of constant change. You change partners; you change jobs, places, patterns, and beliefs. You change in search of what feels right for you. However, no matter how much you change, nothing ever makes you feel completely right. What is right is your reality and nothing of the world of form is reality.

In the stillness of your thoughts, you find reality. In the quietness of the mind, you hear what is right for you. It is there, within you. Your reality is in you. Only, you cannot become aware of it because you are too busy thinking about the outside world and dwelling within yourself. It seems like the mind is running through a plethora of thoughts with every second that could actually be right, not because you think all those thoughts simultaneously, but because the mind is inconceivably fast. You can only have one thought at a time. You cannot see two forms at once. That is why you need to stop and think which thought is leading you.

Marriages exist to continue the thread of special relationships you have previously begun with your parents. Men and women get married to follow a pattern. They believe that with another body they will not be alone. They still see a world outside of them and they separate."

Liliana has held the idea of marriage as something valuable and precious. But, so far she has not found anyone who wants to marry her. She is still young. Only now has she begun to accept the fact that marriage is not reality. She is afraid that if she accepts that idea she will never have the chance to get married. She feels that something is choking her. Antoine notices and asks what is wrong. She starts crying and she cannot respond. Antoine says, "Release that idea because it is of the past. What I will show you will help you to release." He asks her to write down the thought that is troubling her. Liliana writes, "If I am free in the mind there is union so there is no need to get married."

Antoine: "Where is this coming from?"

Liliana: "Me. That's what I think."

Antoine: "So, you are saying that if you release the idea, you will not get married? That is what your mind wants. It is kicking you twice on the rear by keeping you jailed with an idea from the past and in the fear of not getting married. Unwind from those ideas that keep you imprisoned and move forward to do what you want to do. I know it is hard to understand."

Liliana: "I understand but it is hard to release."

Antoine: "Why do you think that is?"

Liliana: "Am I the one making it hard?"

Antoine: "Then, do something about it."

Liliana looks straight into his eyes and says nothing. She feels cold because she knows in her heart that she is responsible for her own thoughts.

Antoine: "Be free within. Think always of the big picture, which is to free yourself. Do not get caught up in ideas that imprison you. If you do, do something about it."

"Humans say that life must continue and that everyone needs to follow the theory of evolution; that it is their duty to pro-create. No one creates; Man only fabricates.

Your children are a gift from the higher source as a spirit, not in their body. They are gifts of their ego-mind, which made their body. They are part of the oath you and they made with the ego. Your child is just another ego-mind that has taken a new form. It is a child of a higher source that fell asleep like you. Your child is your kin the same way your parents and your spouse are your kin.

Your kin is who you are; there should be no exceptions. You are the same as every one and every thing around you. If you say that your children belong to you, you are saying that they do not belong to a higher source. Your children belong to the world, as one with their kin. Your children and you are not bound to those conditions that the ego-mind has set. You are free to join with them and recognize the purity of creation.

If you say that your children are yours, you accept their bodies, you make their ego real and you deprive a higher source from its own children. If you love your children as you say, and if you love yourself, as you think you do, love each other then as pure and sacred spirits of heaven.

To your parents you owe nothing, they are just like you. They are also your kin. Free the burden that you have with your parents for it is not real. Free the chains of guilt that keep you in conflict with them. Free them from their ego and see the innocent child in them. Let go of resentment; there is nothing to resent. Your parents have done nothing to you. It is you, your own interpretation of what you have seen them do. Your ego-mind has chosen everything that you like or do not like. That is why I ask you again, 'Do you still want to keep your ego?'

In the realm of creation, there is no competition. The children of a higher source are one, complete and the same. They share just one feature and that is the love of their creator. They all know the same joy and goodness.

You compete with your siblings. You say you are the same blood with them but the moment you lay your eyes on each other you start a competition. The competition goes along with the race of who does more and who does best. You fight carelessly and you blame one another for what you did not receive.

In heaven, your kin is like you. It is part of you and it is one with you. However, in the ego it is never like that. No one is part of you and no one is one with you. If you really want to see someone as yourself, then see him or her as your holy kin. Do not imprison them to their ego-mind and do not punish them for what they have not done, because what you see in them is who you are.

See yourself and the world as children of the source of life. Share with the world the love that you are. Extend the goodness that is within you. Free your kin from the strings of guilt that tie you in knots of pain. Love is not to keep enclosed in a four-walled room. Love is to share with all."

The students and a teacher in a classroom are affected the same way. The students share with their parents what they learn and the teacher shares his knowledge with all. The lessons are not confined to the classroom.

"In the world, a couple joins to share food, to eat and to rest. The world cannot be ignored. A couple is in partnership to share love and growth and joy. They are together to learn and teach each other how to undo the ego and how to share the love of the heart with the world. Within that partnership, there are rules, as there are rules in the world; like not killing a body, or stealing money.

A partnership between a man and a woman is bounded in respect. To share your love with the world is to extend the love in the mind, not to share the body with others in order to satisfy lust. Partnerships are not to be possessions. You cannot possess nor dominate over one another. You cannot depend on each other nor control one another. You are both of the same mind. You are equal. You are both free and blessed and no matter how intimate you are, you cannot make each other special.

I do not tell you that you 'cannot' do such things because I insinuate to have more power over you, nor do I intend to rule the world of illusions. You have the same power in your spirit that I have. When I say that you 'cannot' do certain things it is because all in heaven communicates love. If you want to be with a higher source, you must recognize creation. To be in the realm of creation you cannot follow the ego.

When you are in a partnership, you must liberate from fear because when there is fear, there is no love. Love does not hurt. Love does not abandon and it does not die. Love is freedom and merriment, it is caring and it is sharing.

When a woman joins with her man in the mind and together they share their truth, then their union is virtuous. When a couple comes together to satisfy their desires, they ignore reality. Wanting to satisfy the body is to satisfy the ego, and the ego is false. Those couples who see each other as independent from the other will stay in fear; only when joining in the heart, fear will vanish from their minds.

Child, learn how to see the light in the world. Receive the gift that they offer to you. Accept them as part of you and be in peace with the whole world. The ropes that knot the special relationships cannot let you be free. Your spirit does not ask you to cut the ropes and end your relationships. It simply shines light on your mind to help you release all the conditions that you have brought upon your relationships.

Once you are free of conditions, you are with the whole and you are free to identify your truth. Let go of all judgments and conditions that you have put on to the world. Unbind them for creation to reveal.

I know that you would think, 'How it could be possible to see your child the same as the butcher,' for example. Your child and the butcher are children of a creator. They are your kin. I do not mean to say that your spouse and your parents should be nil to you. In the dream, while you are in the world of form, they are still what they are to you. It is in the mind and heart that you see them as equal to you, as one with you because that is what they are and you are.

The people in your world should mean to you what a creator means to you and you should love them as you love your creator. Do not become attached to their bodies because their bodies are not their reality. Why would you be attached to what will soon perish? Only in the mind is where you can love infinitely.

Spirit offers freedom. My voice comes from heaven and I communicate to your heart. Those knots of guilt that keep you bound to the ego are not true. You owe nothing to the dream.

What could you owe to something that you made and that is going to die? What could you owe to something that you give power? The ego keeps you hypnotized by telling you that it made you and that it can control you. You will be hypnotized until the day that you wake to reality, the reality that you are not a body but that you are a divine mind. The ego is nothing without your power, not a thing! Nevertheless, you enforce its power every time you indicate humankind as a stranger to you. When you judge a person and you make his ego real to you, you bow to both egos. If you want total freedom of mind, you must renounce the thoughts that caged you in limitations and mortality.

If you want love, turn away from hate. It is very simple, yet you still think it is impossible. The child of a higher source has the power of creation and anything is possible for him, even the undoing of the dream. Until the dream ceases to be special, the ego will lead. If you believe in illusions, you deny reality. If anything of the ego is special to you, you choose not to love your higher source.

I know that my words may seem hard on you but that is only because the ego does not want you to know the truth. It gets hurt easily, right away, and it sets up defenses. The ego is nothing and should be nothing to you. You should see no differences, as spirit sees no differences. The knots of fear and guilt are choking you; that is why you find yourself in despair to breathe, and in despair to have a moment of peace. You do not need to punish yourself for anything. You are guilty of nothing.

The cost of hypnotism from the ego has been very high and you have more than paid the price. The child of truth has all and there is nothing for it to purchase. What the ego has to offer, the child does not need. Do not be seduced with false jewels because even if you polish them, they will tarnish.

The gifts that the ego has for you are illusions of your reality. They are false affairs in what will perish into nothingness. With its plan, the ego does not let you be still. It always brings any sort of events for you to get busy and spiral down in confusion. It also keeps you in endless "doing" so you do not have a moment to think.

You think that it is from your destiny to do what you are doing. Sometimes you call it karma. In truth, the dream is keeping you entertained, busy and distracted.

Without understanding why you are where you are, you follow the dream everywhere it takes you and you blindly agree to everything that it says. The world promises that it will give you what you are looking for, and that it will resolve the meaning of your existence. Your existence is in you and the only meaning to it is within you. Once you recognize that, you live."

In the world, there is a lot to pay off, a lot to overcome and a lot to confront; and many consequences follow. In the real world, however, all is shared and perfect.

"You who are accustomed to difficulties, differences, opposites and extremes, might think that to be in one state of mind all the time would be boring. You would think that to be in perpetual joy would be tiring. I assure you that it is not; the 'ego' makes you feel that. The state of constant joy is your reality. Nevertheless, you do all sorts of things in search of joy, freedom and peace, because you are looking to restore what is truly yours.

If you accept the ego, its false impressions will have control over you. It will obliterate the intention of reuniting with creation; it will make you think that peace is boring and that you will have no joy in the world. How could you not enjoy the world when you __are__ joy? Why believe that to be happy you need to pay the price of sadness? Gaiety is not boring. Imagine what it would be not to shed another tear again.

There is no price to pay for what is already yours. Simply restore what is yours and do not enforce delusions anymore. You already have all that you need. Do not take what you do not need and what you do not want. Your mind is you and it is what you want it to be: the ego or the perfect child of the creator."

Chapter Ten

After the mind fell asleep, it was in darkness where it was lost in a world of form. The mind still maintains that what is real is form. It is hard to disassociate from what the mind has been accustomed to, which is the world of form.

"Without the world you believe to be real, you feel lost. When you remain attached to form, you will accept the dream's ideas as true and you will give up your power. Once your power is given to that world, it then uses that power against you. The body is simply a form that you borrowed from the ego. It is used to carry on the promise of not remembering your truth. The body does not belong to you. It is temporary.

To believe in humankind is to believe in death. Faith in your spirit is faith in life's source. Calling to your spirit is calling to love. In the dream, you are alone because the 'id' keeps you separate from all others. You carry the desire to unite with others but as you come close to them, the 'id' imprisons you in your own self-image and in fears. Sometimes that desire may seem like it will last forever, but regardless of how long it may last, the union of the bodies will perish. How can the mind-asleep unite with others when its decision is to separate? The body will always follow the mind no matter how much you try not to separate from others.

In the world, you do and think for yourself. You seem to be with others but you are always seeking to please yourself. The world seems to be there to help and support you, but in the end you will find yourself alone among your feelings and thoughts. When you are complete, you are never alone; therefore, you never do anything alone. Put your faith in what you love.

I cannot tell you what to choose. What I can tell you is that nothing good has ever come from the world of illusions. If you want truth, simply ask your spirit and your light-mind to guide you. Ask it then to help you decide on your way of existence instead of trying to do it on your own.

In the dream, you will remain confused and never find the truth, but you can trust in your spirit and doubt will disappear since your spirit is certain. The mind-asleep is in doubt. Why trust what is in doubt?

You believe in what you believe because you hope, and hope comes from not knowing. Hope is wishing. It means not having yet wanting to have. You hope for love and good things because you are afraid you might not receive what you hope for. Hope is not certain, and even hoping for the world is hopeless. If you depend on your hope, then you are powerless and you cannot do anything for anyone.

If you mean well, you give. If you love, you share love. There is no need to hope for love since love is already in you. Whatever you mean and what you want to share with the world, you share in your heart where your spirit abides. Hope is an empty word as is the ego. The only word that has substance and is full is the word of a higher source.

The word of a higher source is the only word of truth. It is the only word with meaning. It has no sound for it has no form and no space. The higher source calls to you, but you choose not to listen because you are in a dream world of sounds and forms.

Child, put the games on the side and spend a moment with your creator. Listen to its word and see its light shining through you. Recognize that the creator loves you. Embrace its love with your heart."

Most of the days Liliana feels the heavy burden of sleep deprivation. When she tries to go back to sleep after an entire night of writing she feels out of sorts, and then when she finally falls asleep again, she is drawn into disturbing nightmares. She imagines a world transformed into horror and chaos. She prays for relief but she cannot go back to sleep, yet all she craves is to sleep. Sometimes when the voice wakes her and she replies that she is tired and she wants to sleep, the voice says: *"**Child, you have been sleeping for a long time**."* Liliana says, "Well then, just let me sleep a little longer."

"Why would you want to stay in a world where you seem to have physical pleasures, but eventually they all dematerialize? Love your body as part of you, not as your possession. Love the world with purity and gentleness. See the body with forgiven eyes and accept the spirit of every one in the world. You do not need to search to find what you have been looking for now that you know where it is. Pain and sorrow has just been an illusion.

The ego is just a design. How much do you love it and how long do you want to keep it?

Every memory is a misguiding thought toward the higher source. Every judgment you hold against anybody is a thought opposite of the truth. Judgments are from memories, and memories oppose timelessness. If you really loved a higher source you would be with it. To be with it is to think like it, and not to be in thoughts that are opposed to it. The world calls on a higher source all the time. "Oh my God!" is a statement that humans repeatedly use. If you use a word so much, you love its meaning and you identify with it. If that is so, then there is no doubt that you love a higher source. However, if that is so, then why do you give power to the thoughts that oppose the higher source?

You treasure what you love and you protect what you love, there is no doubt about that. Why then is it so hard to protect the thought of a higher source from the thoughts of the ego? Your mind-asleep made the ego, and you will keep it until you do something about it. Do not fear the ego. It cannot do anything to harm you. It does not know how to harm you without the power you and only you have consigned to it. The designs of the ego can hurt you only if you allow them to. In this respect, you are the only one with the capacity to hurt yourself.

The world is in your mind and you are your own mind so it is up to you to choose what can hurt you. Even what seems to be overpowering you is your own ego using the force you have given to it that is within you. Do not protect what you made. Remember that the ego's only purpose is to distract you from the thought of your source: the thought of love. If you want peace of mind, disregard any attacks. What steals your peace is not what you think happens to you. You are the one that chooses to disregard your own peace."

When we are in love, we soar above the clouds, and we think it will last forever. We think, "This is how paradise feels." However, the ego will not let us keep that sense of love for very long. The ego is relentless. It lets us enjoy love for a little while, but then using the element of surprise, it pulls us down to taste the dirt of its most evil passions.

The union of what we thought was love ends. We then become distracted from ourselves, with pain, and the thought that our heart has been broken. How can our heart be broken when the heart is our mind and spirit? By keeping the thought that the heart has been broken, we feel depressed and we then resent love. Then, no matter how resentful we may feel, we later start looking for love again. We then keep searching for love. But why do we search when love is within us? You are never truly alone.

"The ego will continuously blind you no matter what you are seeking. When you need to turn to your heart where love abides, you turn to the ego by believing that someone or something else will give you what you are seeking. End that ambiguity.

Creation does not need protection from anything; but you need protection from your own ego; and you are the only one who can protect you. Your consciousness gives the ultimate order of what state of mind you want to be in.

For how long do you want your mind to remain asleep? How long will you continue to believe in dreams? How long will you deny the truth? You need to be on guard that you will not be tempted to fall into illusions of sorrow and death.

The "watchman" needs to keep the thief from entering the park, and he needs to stay awake. You need to stay alert to keep an eye on your ego so that it cannot steal your liveliness and distract you from your truth; your truth is peace of mind and unconditional love.

The dream seems to be good for you, but it is not. It seems to give you love and joy; but after letting you play with the fancies of those feelings, it disappoints you and takes everything from you.

Nothing that is false can be good for you. How can something that is counterfeit be used to obtain what is real? Your reality is of a higher source. When you walk with its presence, joined with its mind, nothing of the world of form can do anything to you. You will be free of uncertainties and no fallacies will control you. Unite with your creator by accepting truth."

Following the experiences with her brother and her friend, Liliana is compelled to share her thoughts with the world. Maybe it will accept the message. She is experiencing doubts, though, that she is up to the task of converting her copious journals into book form that she can share with everyone. She tells Antoine of her fear of failure and of her doubt.

Antoine: "Worry is normal. Be in the now and have faith that the voice and our spirit will take care of everything that needs to be done in order to make the book happen."

Antoine is positive of what is to come. He smiles at her to comfort her and he says, "This book is not your idea. It is the voice's, so have the certainty that one day it will be out for the world to read."

"What seems hard to overcome means nothing, especially if what needs to be overcome has no substance. Trust the heart, not the ego, because love is absolute. Humankind promises love, however, there is no need to promise love. You are love, and if you are love, you do not need a promise to love. Recognize the love that you are sharing forever.

Men want to live and love forever. The only way to immortality is to think differently. It is to think before the separation. It is to overlook the matters of the body and its appearance and to acknowledge the mind in sameness with the world.

The attraction of the body is so confused in the world of the ego that everybody thinks it is love. If you truly love, your love will never change and it will never die. The love that the body knows is like a magnolia flower. It is big, delicate, open and white, and before it is time for it to bloom, the petals begin to fall. The magnolia is beautiful but it is never in complete blossom. It is always falling apart. True love never falls apart and never changes. Humanity has the vision of love but not the reality of it. How can love be in the dream when the dream started after the separation from the source of love?"

People look everywhere for love, that is why some people shop for groceries at midnight; They go and they buy things that they do not need, spend money that they may not have, just to eye women. And the women try to impress men with their pretty faces.

"Look at all the things that you do, hoping, wishing, desiring and wanting to find love. Ask yourself just this one question: 'How can someone, who has not found love within; how can he find love and how can he give love?' You need to remember that love is within you, so you can share love, otherwise, how can you give something that you ignore you have?

Your search for love is to find what completes you. Yes, you are loved. In fact, you are love. The bodies that expressed affection may not have loved you; however, the child of a higher source of people, and a higher source itself, will always love you.

In the ego, the love a couple experiences has stages. It has a beginning, middle and an end. How can love have stages when it is infinite? All levels of love have stages, and the most intense stage is that of the honeymoon. The honeymoon is a delusion within the illusion. How can anyone bring the honey to the moon? How can the honey sweeten the inaccessible moon? None of this can happen in reality. That means that the honeymoon is a wish, a fantasy, a contradiction that is unreachable. After the honeymoon, the stages of the relationship continue.

The relationship turns into insecurities, dependency and unreliable comfort, and then it keeps on changing until the love or the gratification dies. If the love had started in the mind, it would not have changed. The relationship changed because the conditions upon the self changed.

Love of the mind is the love of a creator; it is total and unlimited. To love in the mind is to share the body with no conditions but with respect; it is to release the past and find each other's heart in timelessness.

You should probably feel upset or disappointed for being in the illusion of love. Pay no attention to what you feel. The mind can make you feel many things. As you did not remember about true love, neither did any other minds. Your partners have probably been sincere with their thoughts about love, but they did not know that what they felt was not love, but the illusion of love. There is nothing to blame and no one to blame but yourself."

With her head somewhere in space, Liliana leaves her journal unattended. Someone picks it up and reads it. That person who found it misinterpreted her writings, which were thoughts from the voice. A problem arose from that incident and that made Liliana feel very guilty. She has always felt an overwhelming responsibility about sharing her writings, and it is precisely that feeling that has until now prevented her from writing. This episode happens and she vows to stop writing. But once her guilt and insecurity leaves her, Liliana attempts to resume writing if only for the sake of truth and love.

"There is responsibility to take for your choices. Take the responsibility that you have chosen the separation and that in the dream nothing is of truth. Understand that while you have thought you are the person that you identify with, you have not been remembered for whom you really are, but rather for what you have projected upon another person's memory.

Everyone in the world projects what he or she wants you to believe. They are lost in separation and do not remember who they really are. If you keep the idea of love that changes and that dies, it is only because you choose that. There is no one to blame, there is no guilt to feel. The ego does not want you to remember what you know, so you keep seeking love. Now you understand, and the games that have always made you cry can be over in a second if you so choose. The second would be the present, and the present is where your truth is and where you are free of everything that you do not want."

By now, you are starting to understand who you really are and where your reality is. But it is up to you to go there and recognize it for what it is. Remember always, that wherever you are, if you love with your heart, you love a higher source, and loving a higher source is being with it in the realm of creation.

"Loneliness is the most treasured feeling of the ego-mind, and at the same time, it is the most hideous scheme in the world. It is possible to feel lonely regardless of how many people surround you, and how caring they may be. The world is crying in loneliness because every single person, even you, is lonely without a higher source. Loneliness and fear are the two initiators of the ego. Whether you surround yourself with friends or you busy yourself to the point of losing your breath, you will be in fear and you will cry in loneliness if you choose the ego-mind.

The fear towards the creator that the ego inflicted on the mind is so immense that you cannot have the capacity to understand it. You have found yourself thirsty for your truth even though the world has played with the possibility of giving you the truth. However, at the very sight of the light of heaven, the ego will scream, run and hide. The ego will tremble so hard before the presence of truth that the body breaks down. The ego is nothing! It crumbles down and vanishes.

Do not try to imagine how the ego will react as you awaken and you come upon your truth. I have said that the schemes of the ego are beyond your comprehension. That is why you cannot imagine what heaven is like. No pretty picture in the world of form could ever describe heaven. What you can imagine is what you have learned from humankind. For as long as your awareness is in humankind, you are captivated by limitations. Nothing of the ego relates to infinity.

You cannot go to a higher source as humankind. Darkness cannot enter into the light and coexist. Light will dispel the ego completely. You can go to the higher source in your mind, as your supreme mind will guide you. It quietly teaches you about love. It edifies your vision of the world with forgiveness. Your spirit is supreme, and undoes what you know of yourself to find your real self. Your supreme spirit enables you to see in the present, making all things real."

See illustration 2.

<u>Chapter Eleven</u>

On the weekends, Antoine and Liliana like to go on leisurely drives along the coast. They will walk on the beach and sit on the pier even when it is cool and sweaters need to be worn. During one quiet Saturday, Liliana gets bombarded with thoughts from other people around her. She can't seem to control them or to stop them from intruding into her mind. She feels her emotions shifting between happiness and sadness, anger and joy. She pauses and tries to correct her mind but the thoughts keep coming. She asks Antoine what is happening. He explains that during the time she has been hearing the voice, her mind has developed a new, heightened sensitivity to her surroundings. She was becoming empathetic to the emotional state of the world around her. She asked him what to do.

Antoine: "Do not take them."

Liliana: "I am trying not to accept any of these thoughts, but it is like someone is throwing things at me. And I can't seem to stop them from hitting me. Can I build a shield to protect my mind from other thoughts?"

Antoine: "In the mind there is no wall to stop thoughts. The mind is like having a phone. Someone makes a call and the phone rings. You cannot avoid the call coming through but it is up to you to pick up and accept the call or to reject it."

Liliana: "This is constant work."

Antoine: "Wouldn't you rather work for a few years now in order to be saved from lifetimes of pain later?"

"To know truth is to question the dream. The journey to heaven might seem hard only because you think that heaven is not within you. You have been taught to believe only what you see and it is hard for you to believe in what you cannot see.

The ego-mind feels that there is a stranger in its home. It is an uncomfortable, unsettling feeling to which it is not unaccustomed. A beam of light does not exist in the dark. Moreover, for darkness to remain, it must shut out all light. Darkness cannot tolerate light. By definition, darkness is the absence of light. Light and darkness cannot coexist simultaneously.

The ego does not want you to remember yourself because you are light, and in the light of your heart you find truth. It will do anything to distract you from going within yourself. It will jeopardize your thoughts so that you get lost in the idea that only the world that you witness exists. When you start trusting yourself, your ego-mind can, and will, change that trust into doubt. To see light you must look away from darkness. The light of heaven will bring the awareness into the spirit and will open your heart to the remembrance of your source.

The ego-mind seeks to keep the body occupied with a multitude of needs and all its functions. Humankind's actions stand on the idea that the world is moving forward. Nevertheless, all actions are influenced by experiences from the past.

Humankind can only judge a situation from the memories that it has kept through the illusions of time. It responds not to what the situation really is, but to what it seems to be. Your spirit on the other hand, knows of no past. It guides you to your knowing by letting you see each situation differently. It brings you into presence, which is the way to peace and love. The ego can only guide you through complications since complications dwell in darkness."

To relinquish something that we have been part of might not be easy at all, especially when that something happens to be the self. Liliana is determined to release her ego, but she does not find it as easy as she thought it would be. Her ego keeps taking her to painful episodes of fear where her body seems to be taken by a great force and concurrently resists itself. Liliana blames it on the fact that she still falls into judgmental thinking given that she still has to interact with the world. She thinks it was easier for Antoine since he did not have to deal with the outside world.

Antoine: "Yes, it was just me and the voice constantly, day and night since I had nowhere to go. There was no time. It was communication in timelessness. But when I was released, I had to put all I knew into practice. Even though my faith was solid, sometimes it was not easy to detoxify."

"Humankind wants to return home. It is that voice within you trying to help you remember that something in you is not feeling right, and that something in the world is just not good. Men want to find the answer to the world's secrets. They have been waiting for something to happen to give them a sense of home.

How can a child return home when he does not know he is lost? The candle that lights the way to the truth is in you. You have been in darkness for too long and if you look straight at the light, the eyes will go blind. The candle is there to ease the eyes and to comfort them. It soothes them from the piercing depth of the darkness the mind has held. The way to return home is in your hands; you only have to look within and not to your facade.

What comes from a higher source teaches the understanding to its world. How can two different worlds understand each other? The world of form and the world of light and spirit are two different worlds.

You, who are so anxious to know the truth, look out no more. Look within. Heaven is unexplainable. Heaven just is. When you unite with all, and hand-in-hand walk to a higher source, you see heaven and the shining lanterns that illuminate the angels that wait for you. Whatever you have felt in the body that is of goodness and peace cannot compare to what heaven is like. When you return to the remembrance of heaven, you will know with clarity and you will see the truth for yourself. You will not look back, nor would you think of the insanities of the ego-mind. In heaven, the ego is no more.

The body does not need to crave for what is gone. The body denotes a dream. It is not you. It is what separates you from the power of creation. Why remain absent from creation? If you do not love who gave you infinite life, do you value death? There is no middle ground. Either you recognize your knowledge, or you remain in confusion. My words have defined a higher source, and that is who you are. However, if you choose the dream you will be at its mercy and not remember reality.

You have two alternatives: the source of life or the ego. If you are not present with the creator then you value the ego.

Keep only what you love. Heaven wants you to keep what you love. What do you love? Always ask yourself that question and be honest with your response. Why would you want to deceive yourself? Think honestly, why would you want to stay in a dream of sorrow, deceit and death?

The separation has been long and tiring. It has led you nowhere. It has given you nothing. When you try to unite in the mind by refuting the body, the 'id' might feel that it will lose all that it identifies with. Yes, you might lose everything that has brought you misery, but you will gain all. You gain by restoring your power when you acknowledge truth within you.

Think how much you can have if you join with the mind of the world and the angels of creation and a higher source! Your power will be stronger than the world itself.

Release the memories from all the times that you have existed in your ego-mind. They are the chains that keep you shackled to the world of mortality. They keep you immobilized and hurt your beautiful self. Your spirit releases them for you. Ask it, and it will do it with love. It promised a creator that it would light the way for your return. It will hold its promise for as long as a creator is infinite; a higher source is infinity. That is why creation will return when it decides to awaken in spirit. The world of form is unreal. You cannot tire your spirit with questions. You will not bore it with everything that you need, nor with the steady calls placed upon it. Your spirit is your gift to shine light and love. It is there to save you from a horrible dream of pain.

Anything that you can think of, you already have. You have all that you want, all that you can imagine. If you can think of peace, peace is within. You have always had peace. To find peace you have to go nowhere, you have nothing else to do.

Peace is in you. You are peace, but you also are the one who keeps yourself from it. The world cries for peace but it does not want it. People do endless things and keep only the thoughts that hinder their peace. If you really want peace, you can have it now. However, you choose not to have it now because you are afraid of peace. Release the past and with it release the idea of the future. In this moment now, only peace exists.

You cannot make the world responsible for your peace. Only when you free the world from its illusion can you keep the peace that you desire. How can the world bring you peace when its maker does not know of peace? The search for peace will never end. If you keep expecting peace from the external world, you will crash a thousand times, yet each time you will crave more peace.

Why trust something outside of you? Would you not rather trust yourself? The world promises you that it will provide you with peace. It asks you to look for peace but does not let you find it. The world has many things to give but they consist of just one thing, and that is guilt.

Humanity thinks that by stopping war with confrontations peace will come. You can be in peace in the middle of the battlefield. You can march all you want for peace but you will never see peace unless you acknowledge your own peace in the world. What you see is what you project and what you project is who you are, and you are peace. When you are in peace, you are in it with "the all".

You are never alone. You can never be alone when the world is within you, and it goes wherever you go. When you are in the ego-mind, everyone around you, even you are in thoughts of separation, of fear and guilt. If you are in your supreme mind, unity, peace and love is in all. Be still for a while, you do not have to do anything. Be in presence and see the beauty of union and forgiveness. Forgive not what humanity has done, for it has no meaning at all. Forgive the error of choosing the mind of illusions. Forgive the world to enjoy all that you have always been. Be now. It is all that you have. Nothing else is real but this moment.

Be still and acknowledge your creator. See yourself in it. Be thankful for it. Appreciate it all. Thank it for all your gifts. You spend days, weeks and years thinking of just your 'id'. Your creator has given you all that you are. It has not given you oceans for you to drown in it. It did not give you the cold for you to freeze. It did not give you a body to die. A higher source has given you life.

Be thankful now. This moment is infinite. This is where you live. This moment, this "now" in your mind is your reality. When you go back in time, you die given that the ego made time to lead you to death. In your destruction is where the ego exists.

You, who always think in time, do not realize that you are in presence. While you are thinking of the past or fantasizing about tomorrow, you are in the present. Time only exists when you think of time and you think of time to avoid presence.

The world fabricates minutes, hours, days and seasons. Everyone sees their seeming reality reflected on themselves and they suffer as they see their reflections pass from one to another. The passing of time is a reminder that all will be gone.

You are in a constant battle against time. It is a race that steals away your peace of mind and your liveliness. Time has only brought you anxiety and the fear of death. Humanity has made up time and a way to measure it in its mind; and within that, it has seen the world transform itself.

When you accept that time is unreal, and what goes within time is not real either, you will find freedom of mind. To live forever is to be in the present; in presence, you find freedom. The world does stop when you stop time. You can stop time when you stop dwelling in past thoughts and in future fantasies. You have the power to stop what is hurting you and to undo what you have done. Why wait in time? Why would you not correct the mind to the timelessness?"

After a night off from writing, Liliana wakes up feeling completely exhausted, as if a truck had just run over her. She feels drained. She tells Antoine that she feels like she has just been in a battle.

Antoine: "It is a battle."

Liliana: "Why?"

Antoine: "Because the ego is resisting itself. You think that you are sleeping, but your mind is not. Actually, it is constantly shifting from light to darkness and vice-versa."

Liliana: "How is it doing that?"

Antoine: "With all your new understanding, even though you are probably choosing the light, your ego mind always tries to take you back to darkness. It is its nature to do so."

Liliana: "Why do I feel so bruised?"

Antoine: "When the mind goes to darkness, it goes to the memory of pain, anger, sickness… and the body automatically reacts. As the body responds and the mind shifts back again to the light, the body goes into shock, it gets confused. That is why you feel so drained."

"True, you are tired. The world of form will not get better. It will continue to demand of you and it will never have answers. Absolve humankind, free yourself from mortality. Release time from your mind. To be in the body has cost you many tears, and if you want to remain attached to it, the price will only get higher. You will have no choice but to pay. In the dream, there are loans and there are debts. When you cannot pay the price for what you think life is, the body will pass away. It is a contract, and as long as you believe in the dream, you stamp the contract with a validation. The ego gives nothing freely. It sells you gold for the price of your soul. It tries to convince you that you have nothing, so you look to get more from its world. In truth, you have all.

Do you know what all is? All is all. All is everything. When you have all, you need nothing. You want life because you think that you are to die. Your creator extended life to you but you do not remember, for you have chosen to be in the mind that deprives you of life. You are not in your reality so what you ask for and what you want is reality. When you want something, it means that you are lacking who you really are, which is light and love. When you are real, you are wholesome and nothing of the ego will have any effect on you; you will desire nothing, you will remain attached to nothing and you will surpass all limitations.

When you absolve the world of its illusions, everything in the world of perception turns to be the same in its purity. In forgiveness, there are no differences. The desert is no different from the sun. The snake and the shark are kin to you. However, if you see all in sameness, the 'id' may feel that you are indifferent to the world and that you do not care for anyone and anything. By forgiving the world, you become unconditional love.

All the love that you give to the world will grow within you. Forgiveness is peace. Do not wait to forgive. Ask your spirit to shine forgiveness on your kin's ego-mind and on yours. When you forgive, the error of choosing illusions corrects itself. Only a forgiven mind can forgive and only a supreme mind can bless."

Chapter Twelve

Memories are monuments to the past. We recall memories and we choose to retain them because they define our identities. Without memories, we have no point of reference as to who we are. There can be no existence without them.

"The ego-mind believes that memories are your most valuable treasures, so you never let them go. You hold on to them since only the dream can drive you from them. You probably think that only the romantic feelings and the thoughts in your awareness come from memories. However, you do not think that all sickness and suffering also come from the memories that you decide to keep. Even death and the way you die are from your memory.

You have the ability to choose other memories besides those of sickness and suffering. What makes you choose? Why, after understanding the truth of existence, would anyone choose to remain in darkness? Why, after knowing how to heal, would anyone keep choosing memories of sickness? You can recognize that you love what you keep and that you keep what you love. In this case, you keep the memories and thoughts that you want.

Willingness is the determination to decide to act. You have the will to choose which thoughts you want to keep - whether you want to side with the thoughts of the ego or the thoughts of your spirit. Your 'will' directs your mind from darkness into the light.

The mind always has excuses so it will find any reason to settle on its sleep and think that you cannot unite with creation. The mind can make your fear and vulnerability seem out of control. It can make you believe that something has power and command over you.

However, you chose separation and kept choosing the dream. These words will bring light but they cannot make you choose differently. It is up to you."

"Ego attacks," is what Liliana calls those physical reactions, which leave her with an "ego hang-over." After each episode, she lights a candle and takes a shower. But, as weary as she has become of these attacks, she wonders if they ever will end. Liliana never felt comfortable asking Antoine about his experiences as a hostage, but during one evening walk she decided to broach the subject. She wanted to know if, in the process of correcting his mind, he had any physical side effects.

Antoine: "Since I could not even move my body from that sitting position, I was forced to renounce it. After the voice came to me, I remained in the mind level only."

Liliana: "It is not easy to deal with the body, is it?"

Antoine: "Any circumstance brings an opportunity to heal. You have an ongoing set of experiences, so it is wise to take advantage of them all."

"In the consciousness, lies the nucleus of what you really want. Consciousness is the core of the mind. You are not just that body that gets sick and old. You have all the power that you need to say no to sickness and no to death. You have the consciousness and the willingness to choose immortality or mortality. Consciousness chooses the remembrance of your creator. The body does not live forever, but the mind does. Either you can choose to stay in the mind-asleep that keeps you busy in time and has you suffer in pain to keep you from remembering truth, or you can wake to infinity in this moment and free yourself from memories of grief.

Consciousness is not the same as memories. You do not have to go through a stream of memories to get to consciousness. Your consciousness knows who you are but your awareness does not remember. You have the power to go to your consciousness and remember. If you want to stay in pain, if you want to be in distress and die, it is because you have decided to accept mortality as your reality. Go to your consciousness and open up to the truth. It is the way to freedom; it is the door to peace. Do not fear anything. Only in an alien place is where the child thinks he can be hurt. However, in his home he is forever safe.

At home, the child gets to rule. Rules are of the kingdom and the kingdom is of the creator and of the child. By denying the body and accepting the mind, you can accept the rules of the realm of creation and refute the world of the ego. Turn inward. Go there and see. It was the consciousness that decided to split. The consciousness gave power to the will to make the ego-mind, which made the body. You, who see a world of differences and love to compare, compare then what you believe you are to who you really are.

Compare that little body whose heart beats for no more than one hundred years, to the magnitude of your consciousness abiding in infinity. That body, of which you care so much and worry so much, is nothing compared to your consciousness. When you open yourself to your consciousness, you will know how much you want to live and you will choose your truth. You will then take the power from the ego, and nothing from it will be significant to you.

In your consciousness, you see no guilt and no fear; you discover your power.

Fear is not real. Open up to your real self and let the truth reveal itself. The fear of the separation needs to be remembered, faced and released. You do not need to choose the mind-asleep if you do not want to. You are free.

You have the choice to accept that the world you see is just an illusion. The ego will probably make you feel that if you choose what is not of the ego you lose what you treasure in the world. You may feel many things so that you do not betray the promise that you made to the ego. Nevertheless, do not believe in what you feel and do not try to decide on what to do about those feelings, otherwise the mind will spiral down in confusion.

Yes, there is a lot to lose when you relinquish the ego. You lose all pain and all suffering. When you recognize that the world is a dream and you acknowledge a higher source, you leave the place of death and enter the universe of infinite peace."

After long hours of writing, Liliana feels a pain in her shoulder. She gets frustrated and decides to take a painkiller. Later, the shoulder is still throbbing. Antoine tells her to simply release the idea of pain with her mind, but it is still difficult for her to understand. Antoine explains:

Antoine: "When I was held hostage they pulled my nails out and then soaked them in ice water. Imagine the pain! But the voice came to me in one of those moments and told me to remember who I am."

Liliana: "I'm sorry but when the body is hurting, pain is what I feel.

Antoine: "Yes, the body feels the pain. That is how it sends signals to the brain. But it is within the power of the mind to accept the pain or reject it. You have to keep reminding yourself that you are a mind and that you have the power to command your body."

"When you depend on the body and accept the world of form as reality, you deny a higher source. What you accept, you keep, and what you keep, you identify with. If you identify with the world, you bind yourself to limitations. In the world, you associate with what you identify with, and what you identify with is what surrounds you. Out of the world of nothingness, you make up the world from things that you identify with.

Day after day, you exist for those things and everyday is a constant battle to keep the things that signify you and that portray your 'id'. The struggle not to lose anything of your world brings a continuous set of worries in which you are submerged. When you find no way out of those worries, you take that conflict as existence. You feel that you cannot exist without your 'things' so you accept what you see and what you identify with.

Everything in the world is form. That is why you cannot identify yourself with the world of a higher source. If you accept the world of a higher source, you cannot accept the world of form. It might seem hard to choose between two worlds. One is the world of form, which is the one that you are accustomed to. The other is the realm of creation, which you do not remember. However, it is ultimately what you decide to accept, spirit or form.

You cannot be in a room that is both dark and lighted. You cannot face at the same time what is in front of you and what is behind you. What you see as form is a memory. The body is a memory and a higher source is timeless.

Let your consciousness choose. Heal every petty thought of the littleness that makes up your world and all the worries will be gone. Those thoughts and worries are trifles that overcrowd the mind and get in the way of waking to reality. Heal the thoughts of grievance by choosing the light of your spirit. Accept that it is your consciousness. If you want to exchange the dream of suffering, and you have faith in yourself, then you are free. It is your faith that saves you, your faith in the faith of your spirit."

The story of Antoine's torture lingers with Liliana and is very disturbing to her. She feels anger toward the terrorists. She wants to take care of Antoine, to pamper him and treat him with tenderness and softness. Sometimes when she thinks about it she starts crying. Antoine comforts her.

Antoine: "Dear, what you are feeling is of the past and the past is gone. It is not your reality. It no longer exists. Why dwell in something that is no longer here? With the beatings and the isolation, I also felt anger and hatred toward the terrorists. I wanted revenge. I thought it would be impossible to be in the thought of the moment and exchange those feelings for love, since love is forgiveness. But then the voice told me that nothing was impossible if I simply remembered that I am a mind and not a body."

"The dream of suffering will bring you down to wretchedness. It keeps bringing you pain plus everything else that you do not want. Your consciousness does not need to commit. Your consciousness knows. When your consciousness chooses to accept no more dreams, you transcend to a higher source where there is nothing to choose.

In the dream, you go to sleep repeatedly since rest is a condition of the body. In reality, once the child wakes he will not choose the memories of his dreams again. The dream of the world of death will be no more than a thought. When the child joins with a higher source in completion, the dream will be nonexistent.

Who are you really? What do you really want? It is for you to choose. The power that you have is inconceivable to the 'id' that you believe that you are. You, who are terrorized of your own little body and other bodies, will know your power when you accept your truth. The separation is very simple: The child turned away from his creator and fainted into a sleep. It is in the dream that the child thinks he left a higher source. He then made what turned against him and made him think he lost a creator."

Chapter Thirteen

Nothing in the world has meaning unless we give it meaning. If the tree falls in the forest and no one is there to hear, did the tree make a sound? Did the sound of the tree falling have any meaning if no one heard it fall?

"The level at which the eyes observe is where the eyes are situated. With the eyes, you cannot see further than that level, not above it, not behind it, not under it. You can only see from one point to another, for that is how the ego makes the eyes perceive. The ego wants you to project and to see only limitations so that you do not truly see other possibilities. It gave you eyes that keep you blind from the truth. In your mind, you see from a vantage point above and you will see all that there can be. You will see beyond projection and you will know the secrets of the ego-mind's intentions.

If you want power, if you want knowledge, join with the spirit that is within you. Turn away from the ego and depend on it no more. If you want all, choose heaven and choose not to fall back again into darkness and into the illusion called fear. Go without objections until you find totality, where a higher source shares its power with you.

If you stay with the established human traditions, you will never be able to see. You look at what you project and you project the memories of the ego itself. The ego-mind is a mind very confused and it dwells in the dark, so instead of seeing, you look for what you cannot see. In darkness, it is impossible to see light. In illusions, you cannot find truth. Everything that you project, you take back, but with many questions. Moreover, since what you project is against your reality, you cannot find light and truth in what you see. When you want to find the real meaning to what you witness, you become defensive toward it. How can you defend what you perceive when everything that you perceive is yourself?

The meaning that you give to what you perceive only means what you want that perception to mean. The only true meaning to what you perceive is the one that your spirit gives and that is the meaning of love. Remember how fast the mind is. When you focus on something, the mind had already responded to it. The mind takes a memory, and from that memory it gives a meaning to what it has seen. Then the meaning, the awareness and the reaction, is what you respond to.

The world is never wrong and you are never right because neither right nor wrong is reality. If you say that you are right because you think you are right then you are making your thinking real, and judgmental thinking is unreal. If you see wrongness to argue with, you accept wrongness. Who can see wrongness but he who deems it to be wrongness? When you choose your supreme mind, it does not see right or wrong. The supreme mind abides in timelessness where there are no memories to judge what you see."

Every evening is a new evening for Antoine and Liliana. As they cook together, they let the wine breathe and they share their experiences and their thoughts. Dinners are fun. Liliana asks Antoine a question.

Liliana: "Antoine, how come we never left? I thought we split from the source."

Antoine: "We just think we left. Look at the couch. The cushions, the fabric and the base are all the same, just one big piece. Imagine that the cushions are creation and the couch is the higher source. The pillows are on the couch; they don't go anywhere, even if they are asleep. The same is with the truth. Creation is one with the creator but in the sleep, creation thinks it left. In the dream, meaning in our existence, we are split from a higher source, but in reality we are one."

"You will see what you discern with purity, as it would be the first time seeing everything as it truly is. You then will give no judgment and you attack not on your behalf. If you are affected, good or bad, by anything that you witness you have given it power to make it appear as real to you. Different meanings only come from the ego-mind and if you accept those meanings, you let the ego keep you in illusions.

Your sacred spirit is the light that a higher source gave its child to help him awaken. Your sacred spirit is part of the mind after the separation. Creation is who you are: one with a higher source, so there is no need in your sacred spirit. What need is there for a candle when the room is lit? Your sacred spirit helps you heal the memories of illusions and it restores certainty in you. In the supreme mind you will see the world differently, with the eyes of forgiveness and of love. There will be no judgment upon the world since your spirit does not separate you from others as being right and does not judge others as being wrong. It does not see the body. It sees you. It is part of a higher source, and what is of a realm of reality has no right or wrong to compare to. All is the same.

Every moment is a new moment. It is the only moment. In presence, there is no pain or sadness, for pain and sadness only come from memories. In presence, there is the grace of a higher source. You would think, 'How

could I live in presence if I have tomorrow to think of?'
There is a tomorrow in the world of form. Dinner cannot
be ready if the cook does not think what to prepare after
lunch. Nevertheless, while he is cooking the meal he
should not be thinking of the guest to come. He should not
project his fears and past onto the future. Instead, he
should join with creation. Presence is not in the body. It is
in the mind.

You are still in a body and you cannot ignore the
dream. You have made a world of time and while you are
still in the world, you have to think in terms of time.
However, since that world is not your reality, you cannot
put your trust in time. In the world of time, there is a
tomorrow to think of but not to worry about. Tomorrow is
already given, and it will be solved as it comes. What your
spirit teaches you is that there is no past to hold on to and
no future.

In the world of changing forms, there is nothing to
lose. However, if you choose the ego-mind, you have a lot
to lose. You will lose all your power and all your
knowledge. If you are in a confrontation, remember, what
the other person is doing to you only means what you want
it to mean. Since it can mean nothing to you, you can
respond with nothing, and so you keep your peace of mind
and your power. Power comes from a higher source. When
you know, you know your power and you do not belittle

yourself to the nothingness of the ego. The ego is spiteful. It has too many masks to hide its many tricks.

The more you turn to your spirit, the more you learn. Every moment, every experience is an opportunity for you to learn. The more that you loose the bondage you have with the ego, the closer you become to the truth, and truth is your freedom. You cannot learn on your own because what you know now is of the ego, and you need to unlearn what you have already learned. Truth grasps the truth when you are completely one with the whole. As humankind, still in the dream, you must learn from every moment that you experience in it. You will learn not to be better in the dream, but to undo the dream and to heal from the illusions of fear. Perception is of the body and the body is of the ego. What you see and what you project is an opportunity for you to heal.

If you do not use this moment to heal and learn, you hand over the memory of that moment to the ego-mind to use it later to attack. Use every temptation that the dream persuades you with as an opportunity to learn from it. Even when you think you have failed by choosing judgment and accepting suffering upon yourself, use that 'falling' as an opportunity to strengthen your mind and choose against mortality. Change the dream by healing its memories.

With its memories, the mind will surely remain in scarcity instead of joining with a higher source. Every moment is a moment for you to heal from the dream and get closer to truth. It is for you to wake from illusions and be in reality. Take the responsibility for having chosen an idealistic essence of yourself instead of your true self. By taking responsibility, you can correct your choices. Any emotion that you keep, any memory that you treasure, and any defense that you give, is you accepting illusions.

The more you understand of the truth, the more your power grows in you. But, if you think that you know all and refuse to learn from every moment of the world of illusions, even if it is your last breath, you say that your spirit does not know and that you know more than the source of life.

Thinking that you know all is arrogance. Accepting that you do not know all is humbleness. If you are with a higher source, you can only be humble, for you would not accept any of the teachings from the ego. When you are with a higher source, you are powerful. Truth is knowledge and knowledge is power. A wheat branch stands erect if it has no seeds. A branch filled with seeds bends from the weight of the seeds. However, when the storm comes, the erect branch breaks, and the one bent bows with the strong winds and will not break.

The seeds of knowledge protect the branch of wheat. If you think you know, it means you do not know. When you know what is true, you do not need to defend *what you know; you know it is the truth. The child of a higher source does not need to defend what is not of truth. What is not of truth is nothing. If you say that you know and therefore need to learn no more, then you say that the 'id' is right and that a higher source is wrong.*

The only way to learn and to correct the mind is to be humble. However, humbleness is what the ego detests. You might think you are humble by giving sweets to the poor. Humbleness is to accept nothing of the ego. It is to see everything the same as you, as part of you. It is to say that you know nothing of the world of mortality and to let your spirit guide you to see the truth that is in you and in all. He who is humble learns and he who learns accepts.

Acceptance is knowledge and knowledge is power. Nothing of what you learn from illusions is from the truth. Therefore, what you thought you have learned from the world of memories and form is biased and untrue. You have been convinced that you know, and from that, you have been arguing with the world about what you consider to be right or wrong. You have tried to prove your opinions, which in truth you cannot prove; they are ideas of an illusion."

The most favorite word we use is "I" which is humankind or the "id" within us, the ego. It is our identity and the self we believe we are. Every time we say "I", we nourish our mind-asleep, which pulls us towards the separation. When we say "I", we open the way for the memories to come into this moment for judgment to be justified.

When we say "I," we leave the present and we enter into the past. We validate every single trait from the identity that the ego formed and that we accepted in not remembering our higher source. When we say "I", we separate the identity from the whole and we lose our power. We also find ourselves alone. Humankind wants to isolate from all. The ego puts us in that little "I" world and leaves us there alone to defend ourselves from the attacks of an evil and sick world.

"All responses that you have to everything that you witness is to defend that little 'I' or 'id' in which you believe that you are. When you are in a conversation with a person, nothing but that 'I' follows what the other says. He does the same to your response because he has his own memories shaping his 'id'.

The meaning that you give to the 'I' is from the ego. What is from the ego is not real and nothing that is real can be unreal. Only a higher source is real. You are so used to the 'I' that without it you would feel unguarded before the world. That 'I' is your favorite garment for as long as you accept the ego and want to stay absent from reality.

Would you let that letter lead you more into ambiguity, or would you let the whole save you from the littleness and the misery of limitations? It is your choice. Bring your awareness into those words. They are insignificant to your confusion. Those words help you choose between the force of the self and the power of a higher source. If you let the 'I' go, and if you join with all, you will see the power of yourself leading through you. Remember, what the words say is what it is in the mind. If you say or think all, it is obvious you are with the whole. Do you want control, or do you want elimination and separation?"

To remember a higher source, we must release everything that we thought we were. You may feel that you have been living in a world of lies and deceit. The ego's satisfaction is in the middle of our confusion about knowing the truth. It can purport to be the innocent victim while we remain blind.

"Do not become upset. You did not know the reality of your world. You have been lost. You have been in darkness. You and your kin as well are under a spell of the ego-mind. Do not blame yourself for choosing unreality.

You were fearful, thinking of leaving the creator, such as a child leaving home prematurely without knowledge of direction."

If you choose to eliminate lies and deceit and seek the truth, adjoin with your spirit. It will show you the truth.

"The dream gives you good things, those that you want and that you like, for you to have a happy moment. Happiness is a glimpse of reality. In the world, happiness is not complete, nor will it last. The mind keeps you going from one feeling to the other and from every sort of emotion. It keeps you in a state of daze. It gets you confused, going from one wish to the other. The ego does not care whether you cry or laugh. It gives you pleasure in the body and the good things that you like for you to make your existence appear as real, and to be attached to where you are. It then brings misery for you to fear a creator.

The ego has a plan behind everything, and that plan is to let you down so that you turn back to it. When you are down, either physically or emotionally, you turn to humankind for help. That is what you have been doing for very long since it is what you have known while you have been lost in the thought that you are humankind. When your hopes fall apart, you run to what you are familiar with, and everything that you have learned is of the dream.

The only thing that is not of the dream is your supreme mind; that is where you do not turn to illusions."

Chapter Fourteen

After so many changes happening so fast, sometimes Liliana feels that she cannot even recognize herself.

Liliana: "Why me?"

Antoine: "You always questioned everything and you were always searching for the truth. You were willing to listen. The voice knows that you can do this because it knows you."

"Truth is in your heart, and in your heart is the source of life. It is your responsibility to choose truth in order to be free from the world of suffering and death. Deliverance is the correction of your mind. Deliverance is accepting reality since what you need to be free from is non-reality. It is your own responsibility to decide against non-reality, for it is what you yourself made and what you make yourself believe. You accept what you believe and you believe that there is a truth behind what you have learned. What you have learned are ideas from the mind in darkness and from the mind that believes in humankind. You do not know the ego-mind. You cannot see it. The body

is what the ego-mind made to survive and to block a higher source. To humankind, the ego is important. To creation, it is nothing.

You still do not understand the games of the ego-mind and that is why you cannot discard it by simply thinking spiritually whenever it is convenient for you. The way to renounce the ego is by turning to your supreme mind. You need your spirit to lead you through your indulgence until you are complete, at least until your mind can control the ego with the power of your love.

If you try to understand what the ego is really about, it will confuse and distract you, drawing you toward what attracts you most, your weakness. It will even let you think that you are in truth. When you are in reality, you are in timelessness and knowledge. If you say that you cannot live without memories or the traits that separate you from the rest, then you are saying that you cannot live without the ego. That means that you choose limitations and mortality rather than freedom. You would then not know who you really are.

For as long as you depend on the body, you identify yourself with humankind. When you identify with the body, you are certain that sickness is real; that you are at the mercy of sorrow and that you are going to die. The more you pledge that you are a body, the more confusion you bring upon yourself. I know that as humankind, it can be *difficult not to make the body real but if you accept form and you believe in it, you do not accept your source of life.*

The ego's game is very clever. It has blinded humankind for ages. However, it is true that you made the ego and that you bestow your power. Now, do not think that it will be easy to dominate it and put your command upon it. When the ego made the body, it outsmarted you and imprisoned you in a form of incredible limitations. It has had control over you by making the body and the world of form believable to you.

Before you can relinquish the ego completely, you first need to understand what you see is not real. Then, you should be willing to accept your spirit's teaching and guidance every moment. By shining its light onto your understanding, you will be able to learn the ego's dynamics. Those you must learn and accept as well. To know the ego's dynamics is to unmask the truth of sickness, unhappiness and death. You might be fearful at first, for fear is prevalent in the world. At the sight of exposure, the ego thinks it can hide, but in the mind there is nowhere for the ego to hide.

The ego's dynamics are to extend the journey that requires a lot of dedication and trust. Learning of the ego releases the knots that it uses to keep you bounded to pain and to the dream of death. You will begin to heal your mind and understand the differences between being the child of a higher source and existing as humankind. Healing brings the concept of limitlessness into your awareness. It makes you see with your mind and it liberates you from the sentence of the body for you to find infinity. The healing of the mind takes a lot of willingness, since the ego's plan is for you to not learn of it and figure it out. It wants to keep you devoted to its own functions by keeping you in darkness.

The only way to knowing is by learning. In addition, you need to learn of the mind to know that you are knowledge. You cannot keep relying on the dream if you want to utilize the knowledge that already is in you. I know that you want to remember knowledge. Knowledge is the power that a higher source extended to you when it created you."

This message is not for you to change your beliefs. It is for you to remember the truth that is in you, to choose your deliverance. This advice is to accelerate bringing light into your life, to show you that you are creation and not a mortal human. This message gives us the answer to questions that we have only within the ego. The world believes that it has the secular answers for everything. If so, why then do we keep searching for the ultimate truth? Why do we persist in such a quest if it is not for the spirit that helps us?

"Not believing in anything outside of yourself and yet believing in yourself is what all parents ask of their children, as I do of you. Trust yourself to find the answers. Believe in yourself. Your mind has the ability to teach you if you allow it to. No one can compel you to do anything that is not in your best interest. No one can manipulate your mind if you do not let them; your mind is synonymous with me, as your kin and a higher source. You have your own consciousness.

When I speak of the ego-mind, I do not mean to attack humankind. I only have one meaning and that meaning is love. If you feel offended, it is your own mind having you judge how to feel. Do not accept as true what you feel. Remember, feelings are of the body; they come from a memory and memories are not of reality. The child of a higher source does not understand feelings. A higher source is cause, and a higher source is how the child is. The child has only one memory and that is the memory of its creator. Spirit cannot attack because it knows of no attack. Attack is only of the ego and spirit does not see the ego. You are still innocent. You do not know why you defend yourself from what spirit conveys with these words.

You are the ego's hostage. It is holding you prisoner to keep its rule and maintain its existence. However, there is no ransom, for what you give to the ego is everything that it wants. That is why the ego will not let you free. Only you have the ability to find the way to be free. There is a key to your 'self' and it is hidden where you least expect it. Your spirit is the key that you have been looking for. It tells you about the barrier and how to get around it so you can be free from what keeps you captive.

The mind thinks that it needs to take the world seriously; that is why it does not remember its own reality of joy, love and peace. The ego gave and took away your time to not rest so that you cannot have a second of peace. It makes different forms for you to be distracted in the pattern of wanting and receiving. But the more that you receive, the more that you need to work hard to keep what you have acquired, and to acquire the possessions that you want. The world is a busy and restless place, and everyone thinks that everything that it wants to accomplish is necessary.

However, after everything you do to get what you want, there is nothing left after you die except your mind and your spirit. Where do they go? You will think that what you do will bring you happiness during the time that the body exists. Question that. Think to steady your inner being for understanding.

The world's demands are keeping humanity from the present. Everyone has an ongoing battle with him or her self and they think that perhaps later they can think about the creator. People think that somehow, one day, things will change and they will be up in the sky among the clouds in bliss. Well, heaven is now, in the mind. The ego loves to procrastinate to avoid this present moment. It thinks of the future to keep the past alive, and the past is its continuity."

The glittery events of Hollywood do not concern Liliana anymore, but she does care that her friends from that struggling world are upset with her. They tell her that she has betrayed her dreams of becoming an actor by trading her passion for a "comfortable life". Liliana feels they do not understand the hard work and the difficulty she is going through. "It has not been an easy assignment and it was something I could not refuse." She secretly wishes that one day they will understand and accept her for what she is doing instead of regarding her new life's work as outlandish.

"You think that your sacrifices will compensate you tomorrow. You wish that one day, when you decide, everything will be balanced and that you will have peace and happiness. You think that when you get this or that, or when you are here or there, you will find peace and love. The world pretends to sell peace and love to you but when you get home and open the package, you only find an empty box. Completion is here and now.

To find love, close your eyes and look within yourself. Do not wait for humankind to bring you what you are searching for. You are the only one who has the will to obtain what you want.

When you anticipate, you expect something to happen. You anticipate because you guess, and you guess because you do not know. The love that you find within you is nothing like the fancies that you have felt in the body. It is an unconditional love that shines in purity. It is a love that completes you. Look within yourself and find the love that lifts you from the body and has you floating through the infinity of heaven. When you get a glimpse of love, when you get a taste of the peace that is in you, you will not run out to pay a high price for an empty box that the world wants to sell to you. Look into your heart and worry no more about tomorrow. Be total with the love that you find within you. In your heart, you find your truth and you will know there is nothing that is not real.

The spirit offers you love. It is that love that everyone in the world has and that increases in you when you see them all as part of you, as equal to you. Your spirit will not guide you to a place that you do not know. It only takes you home. You may be afraid to look within yourself and let yourself go through those colorful ways that take you right to serenity and harmony. Your 'id' is afraid to confront you. You, who want freedom so badly, are afraid to be free. You still do not understand the rules of the ego, its conditions and the costly games that end with death.

The ego cannot conceive of the thought of total freedom. It lets you wish, and asks you to give your time for a tiny bit of freedom. Humanity does not know how to be free. It does not know if it really wants to be free because the ego does not know of freedom. Men remain jailed to the limitations of what they need and to what they should do. How can the mind be free when a thought disturbs every passing moment of a hectic existence?

The mind is freedom itself, and you can set yourself free, but only for as long as you want freedom. You are the one who chooses to keep the thoughts that make you feel how you believe you feel. You are responsible for the pain, the sadness and everything that you feel. No one can tell you how to feel or what to think. You are of your own mind and you keep the thoughts that you want to keep.

Open your mind and think of this: A thief can come and take things from your home, and the gardener can plant seeds in your yard. But, how can anyone steal your thoughts or put thoughts into your mind? You are the owner of every memory that you have and every thought that you hold. No one is stronger than you are. In the mind, you choose to believe in the body. Those who seem to have a powerful mind simply accept less limitations of their body."

During the day, Liliana can be as normal as those who simply sleep throughout the whole night. Most nights, as soon as her own head hits the pillow, she falls into a deep sleep. On one of those sleepy nights, though, her body begins to shake. She wakes up feeling that something beyond her is taking control. She grabs Antoine's hand and asks him what is happening.

Antoine: "It is your mind. You are doing it to yourself."

Liliana: "Here we go again. How can it always be me?"

Then as suddenly as they started, as she ponders what he has just said, the shudders stop.

"Humankind has a long list of what is right and what is not right. From your birth, you do not know any better, so humankind teaches you what to think and what not to think. You then can accept as true what you learn. When the ego brings you back into another form, it brings you in unawareness so that you do not remember that you are a mind and that it was your decision to choose that body. Raise your eyes child. See the higher cause and how the mind in fear stays in fear.

With your imagination, you can do anything that you want. You can do an infinite number of imaginary things and you can never be limited. If your imagination is in your mind, what then is your mind? You are the artist who draws every thought. What you presently remember is of the ego-mind, which complicates your understanding. Renounce the ego and renounce your 'id.' Imagine the possibilities.

When you renounce the ego, you will not depend on the body or on anything outside of you. When you accept truth, the body is guided by the power of heaven as you become one with the creator and creation."

Chapter Fifteen

Many of us would not have accepted the transformation of our world as easily as Liliana did. Even though she is grateful, she feels that it is a drastic change. One day she feels suffocated and in search of freedom so she decides to drive her car along the Pacific Coast. She opens the windows and even with the sun shining and the wind blowing through her hair, she feels caged. She calls Antoine hoping he can ease her anxiety.

Liliana: "No matter where I am, the house, the car, the gym, I feel as though I am in a box. I feel like a bird with no wings. The writing is taking so long, and it's so hard to understand. I don't want to be closed up inside those four walls anymore!"

Antoine: "Why not rather go into your mind instead of going to yet another ego state?"

Liliana: "I'm sorry. I can't believe I just said that. Even if I never leave the house again, it will never compare to what you went through during your time as a hostage."

"*Realize that within the mind abides the thought of fear toward the creator, and that fear leads the world to discrepancies. Heal fear and remember the realm of creation. Disown the ego. Nothing will change in the world of form except that it will be harmonious and peaceful. If you depend on the dream, you end in oblivion. In that world everything dies, and what dies turns to nothingness. Misery and pain are handouts from the ego. You believe a higher source has given you death. A higher source only knows of equality.*

The world has written many words about reality; all the things you've heard about what we believe is true. Nevertheless, as your awareness is still in the world of form in all its sensations, and in responding to humankind, you still do not recognize a higher source. You believe in a higher source. However, as the child of a higher source, which you are, you have the right to know your creator, not just to believe that there is one. Know your creator. Ask your spirit to lead you back to the remembrance of your truth. You are a child, innocent and sacred, and you always will be. No matter how old men grow or how many titles they hold, the reality of the world can never change.

In the world of the ego, people who run armies and carry gold think they are powerful. Those who cure the body from sickness think they are the saviors of the world. Those who study the mind within the confused mind think they know all. Those who pray day and night think they are holier than those who satisfy their flesh. In truth, his or her ego knows of nothing, it saves no one; it is in guilt and it is powerless.

Humanity can only pretend what it wants to be. The child of a higher source is a child, a sacred child, who is powerful in his totality, and who saves the world from its misery and its errors. That child hides behind the suits that you put on everyday to pretend to be whom you are not. Give yourself the chance to be yourself and get all that you want. To be free is simple; it is to let go of limitations.

You, who no matter how many other bodies you have around you, still think that you are alone. You are never alone. Your spirit goes where you go, guides you and shows you the truth. It cares for you and it loves you. Spirit is even in the grains of sand that burn in the desert. It has been their choice to take the form of sand, but they have not been alone. You still think that you are a body; you speak, laugh and cry; you think you are the only one with a brain. In fact, you are a mind, and behind the river and the rocks; the clouds, grass, lakes, and rain and everything that you see, there is a mind, and that mind is the child of a higher source. In addition, if you love your creator, you love them all the same.

Everyone is always concerned with the problems of their own lives. If you only think about your 'id', how do *you think you will find the truth that belongs to you? Think of all always and your problems in the dream will untangle themselves.*

Let your pride down. Pride is shameful. Pride limits you. Pride is of the ego. Pride does not let you see the truth. It does not satisfy your heart with peace and it would never let you find freedom. If you look down on people, know that whom you look down on is just like you - is one with you. Humankind portrays disparity. It plays with identity, which is what separates one from the other, which is what keeps the world from reaching truth.

Your world is a mirror of yourself. What you see reflects who you are. Remember that always. When you are looking at something, you are looking at yourself. What you see in it is what you want that to be, and you can only want what is in your mind. If you give it a name, a meaning, and judge it, you are separating it from you. You are then in the mind that separates and judges. Think of a lion, would you fear it, run and let it kill you, or, would you rather join with his mind and play with him through the slopes of the mountains? You live in a world of mirrors and they are all around you."

After taking a shower, Liliana looks at herself in the mirror, and for the first time she acknowledges that her body is not real. It was not easy coming to this understanding.

Something in her made her want to cry as if she had lost something of value – as if she had been abandoned. But then quite suddenly an unexplainable sense of freedom came over her. She had finally begun to understand the power of release.

"Creation is incomplete without all. To complete is to join, and joining is completion. Completion is creation. The child cannot wake and still leave part of himself in a dream. Either he is awake or he still sleeps. The ego believes in separation and for that reason, you cannot love all and not love yourself. Humans think they love themselves by believing that they are a body. They are in fact, obsessed with their body because that is all they believe they have. The 'id' tries to convince itself that the body is perfect, that it is a shelter. How can a body be perfect when everyday it grows older and it changes?

Your own mind made your body. You are the one who keeps your body different. You look at your body and you do not like something, so you coerce the mind to think of perfection. No body is flawless. Release yourself from the thought of the body and you will find perfection in you.

No matter what your form or body is; the mind will not be satisfied. It made the body specifically as it is, so when you compare your body to another, your mind does not allow itself to appreciate its form, therefore, you become disappointed. When you measure it you will not find integrity."

How many times have you given something and gotten nothing in return? You have given the world everything that it has wanted and you are still waiting for your reimbursement. Throughout existence, we can settle on the same merry-go-round of expectation and deception when we serve the mind that has nothing to give.

When we follow what the world has to say about who we are; what we are supposed to do, and how the world should be, we listen to the ego. When we accept the world of form and humankind as reality, when we accept anger, sickness, sadness and death, we bow to the ego. When we follow the conditions of the world, we follow the ego's guidance. When we think that humankind is to give us what we want and to give us the answer to our uncertainties, we put our trust in the ego. When we give to the ego, we lose ourselves.

"Nothing is imposed upon you. Your will is your own. If you want deception from humankind, it is your choice to be deceived. You have the ability to give nothing to the ego by bringing light into darkness. No one can force you to do anything.

I cannot force you to return your awareness to the realm of creation. My love guides you to help you remember your truth. When you get tired of dwelling in the insanity of the world and when you get weary of regrets, you will know what you need to do. You will remember your truth. You will see the truth through your eyes as you dismantle the ego.

The ego disguises itself in many ways for you to respond to its functioning, but you have the will that a higher source extended to you. Your will is the will of the creator. In addition, it is in your will to choose between the world of dreams and the realm of creation. It is your will to choose to live in love or to rely on differences.

You always have your spirit in you, waiting for you to ask it to guide you and show you the light of the forgiven world. Blessed are you, child. The light is illuminating you and you can see the world with the light in your heart. The differences of the ego and its evilness are nothing to be afraid of or to be resentful of. What has passed is gone, and the only thing left to do is to correct your mind about your mind. Negative feelings only come from the memories of pain; therefore, if you still feel anything but the grace of a higher source, you are still choosing the dream.

Dreams can only mean something to the dreamer who believes in them. Since the mind made the ego in a dream state, the ego and its world is a dream state. The ego pretends to be compelling. In reality, the ego is just a thought of fear, and you have the power to forsake fear whenever you want. However, that power in you scares you because power is the higher source. You are a mind and you can think anything you want. That is what the world always does.

The world is a painful place to be in, but you still do not think it is. The world is the manifestation of every mind's thoughts. It manifests sickness, sorrow, terror and discrepancies, but not one thought of peace and love. Everything that derives from the ego-mind is to enforce the separation, to keep its illusions real and to confuse humankind from the truth that its reality is a pure and infinite spirit.

To manifest your reality onto the world, which is love, do nothing but turn to your spirit and let it shine away the confused thoughts of humanity. Be certain of your spirit's omnipotence. It will shine on anything that is not light; it will tame the ego, even if the mind pretends to divert from the light by dwelling in its unbelievable designs.

Mind is all there is, that is why every thought is a manifestation. Your circumstances are the projection of your thoughts. You are where you are because you have given yourself everything that you want and do not want. The ego has taught you to see "outside the box", and make the world responsible for your conditions so you never question that your own mind is responsible. You then think that you are fortunate if one day you seem to be happy. On the other hand, sometimes you cry tears of poverty. The ego uses what you value to control you, either by taking it away from you or by keeping it for a time so you will not remember your reality."

The world has many styles of living, from rich to poor, colorful to simple. They are the same. What is different is that each one is a different way of projecting fear. The world gives a different meaning for each way of carrying out an existence.

The king in the palace and the peasant on the farm are both condemned to their own guilt. The crown of the king and the food taken from the peasant's hands are wishes they have taken for themselves. The king projects his guilt on his banquets. His fears are revealed in his solitude; that no one in his world wants anything but riches and security from him. The peasant wants the world to feel sorry for him, and he comforts his guilt with the hunger in which he sleeps.

"Humankind always throws the stone, then hides its hand. It believes in hiding to prove itself innocent, and it thinks that everything can hide. Every thought of what you have seen or sensed stays with you if you hold on to it. The thoughts that you hold will go with you wherever you

decide to go. Those memories remain in the mind by choice until they surface by your preference.

The mind uses memories as a shell to protect the body against everything it projects. That is how you come to attack and defend. As a limited mind, the ego feigns to keep its thoughts hidden, but there are no thoughts to hide. The mind is one and it has no blankets to hide anything. When you are in any circumstance, your awareness is in the response of everything that you are sensing and perceiving. Therefore you are not aware, as others are not aware, that everyone's thoughts have already been shared and that you are already responding to each other's thoughts.

The body is just a mass that responds to the thoughts of the mind. You hide and live with secrets, but there is nothing to hide and there is no thought that is ever gone. Mind reads mind.

You are in either love or fear. Wish for love, think in love and you get all the goodness that comes from love. Any thought that derives from the mind-asleep is a thought of fear and guilt. The ego-mind is a dual mind, and within its differences lies the insanity of the world. Your truth is not the thoughts that are always wandering in your mind. Your truth is one singular thought.

Chapter Sixteen

"*Sickness is not caused by the body. The body in itself is neutral; it cannot function on its own. Every part of the body receives orders from the mind, including the brain that controls the senses and the character of the body. Sickness can only come from the mind that chooses to be sick. The body is to wear out as it progress through its life cycle until it disintegrates. What it feels and what happens during the time of its existence is the projection of thoughts in fear.*

The body is the place of safety for the ego-mind. Therefore, it is necessary for the ego to make the body appear as real in order to justify its existence. What the body has seen, heard, touched, and sensed, the mind recalls as a memory and then reveals it through the body. Truth is now and now has no thoughts of time. The mind is constantly busy with many thoughts; one follows the other and the body responds.

The acknowledgement of pain is the awareness of pain and is therefore the acceptance of it. If you do not feel pain, it is because you do not think of pain, but you need to think of pain to feel pain. The body cannot feel unless the mind first accepts the thought that defines the feeling. If the body feels sick, it means the mind is keeping the thought of sickness.

The mind accepts the thought that chooses sickness. Then, by projecting the thought, it makes itself forget that the thought has been of its own making. Once the mind accepts the thought of sickness, the body responds. Since your awareness focuses on the pain in the body, you do not realize what you are feeling has come from the mind. You then blame the pain on something that you think is outside of you. You put the cause of sickness on the external world, not within yourself.

The ego-mind will never let you know that it is the initiator of sickness and it is the one that chooses how and when to get sick. It made the body susceptible to the conditions of the external world. It punishes the body for its own desires and makes it dependent on it for what it does not know. If the mind knows that the pain or illness comes from the thought of its maker, what do you think the mind will do? The mind will correct itself and choose sickness no more. That is why men believe the world makes them sick.

The source of sickness is in the mind-asleep choosing to punish itself. In the dream, humanity is baffled by the cause. Would a creator do that to its child? Would a father do this to his child?

This is how the mind fools itself: The body is susceptible to the cold wind. If you expose the body to the cold wind, you get sick from it. You then blame the wind for what you feel. In your idea of the world, the mind assumes that a higher source created the wind; therefore, the cause of the wind and the cause of the body becomes the cause of the sickness. In truth, the wind is its own ego-mind. The wind is in your mind and you decide in your mind what it can do to you.

You choose the pain that you feel by what you have seen and have experienced in your world. If a mind has heard of a certain plague or sickness, the mind can use that memory, and in that same way make the body sick. You have the power to choose differently from sickness by correcting the idea of sickness in your mind.

Sickness is a memory. The ego is guilt. Healing is not of the body. Healing is of the mind; it is correcting the thought of fear to the thought of love. It is the acceptance of truth, which frees the mind from the conditions of the dream. Healing is releasing the memories of guilt and the thought of fear.

When the body is ill, it will remain ill until the mind accepts healing. Sometimes you may think that you want to heal but then illness continues. You go to different means to cure the pain and you might get confused as to why you cannot heal. The mind choosing sickness is afraid of accepting healing. To accept healing is to accept the supreme mind, the mind of a higher source.

Accepting healing is bringing the sick mind to timelessness where there is no guilt and no memory of sickness. The supreme mind is the mind that sends orders to the body for the body to correct itself. How fast you accept healing and how fast the body heals is the mind's choice, your choice."

People think that the doctor or the therapist heals them. Their faith in a person or in a certain thing makes them accept the healing. When a patient goes to the doctor, he is already making the decision to heal. If the body continues its condition of illness, even after the person had sought the cure, the mind is afraid to accept the healing. Could this be the reason that the "placebo affect" works, because our mind has accepted the fact that a particular cure will work, when in fact, what caused the cure to work was only a suggestion?

"The mind ignores the present. When the mind responds to the senses, it responds to past. Humankind revolts against presence. It does not understand presence since its existence is in its memories.

See the light of a higher source in your mind and in other minds, for that is where healing takes place. You still believe in the body and you think that is the world in

174

which you exist. Since you love what you believe, you seek immortality. Thus, in the body, infinite life can never be. Let the plan of the body go. Relinquish the thought of mortality.

The mind is infinite. The ego-mind will be there until you let it go. Open your eyes and see with your mind. You are a mind, and the mind is what sees.

Time is an illusion. It is an invention. It is part of the ego's scheme to keep you trapped in the memory and to make you believe that you are just a body. In time, the body gets old and dies. The ego confuses you with time, yet you believe in time profoundly. Yesterday you were a child and now your body is older. What happens to time after the body is gone? Time keeps you away from the present. In the present, no illusions exist.

You may think that you are going forward; but in fact, you are facing toward the past. You may think that you are in the present when you are actually in thoughts of the past. Or, you are only thinking of the future, which you can only do from memories from the past. The ego made time to oppose the infinite. Time is of the body, as is every other desire that persuades the body to appear as real. The mind knows of no time for it is timeless. That is why, when you know you are a mind, you live infinitely.

When you depend on the body, you bind yourself to its limitations. You consider the world as mighty and you make yourself vulnerable to everything it can do. You whirl around the problems of the world and the needs and demands of your body. You fight and attack for what you believe is yours and what you think the right thing should be. The ego distracts you by keeping you busy in getting all the things that you desire. It makes you devote your desires to one body but as you picture the one person you want, then you leave the rest of the whole world thirsty for love. Those things that you remain attached to, and that you work so hard to get, are not real.

Humanity claims that to find reality it needs to learn something that it does not know. The mind cannot forget what it knows and what it is now. It is impossible to forget a thought. You think thoughts are forgotten, but as painful as the memories are, or sickness is, the mind is able to recall all its thoughts at any time. Your spirit is the light in you that shines on the memories that the mind is settling on.

The child of a higher source is perfect. Nevertheless, in the dream, the child of a higher source becomes humankind, which is not perfect. You need nothing of what you think you need. Embrace your heart and share with the world all that there is in it. The more you give, the more you keep and grow. When you share love with all, you accept truth and accepting truth is denying sickness.

Everything that the body does is to project and protect the fears, and to hide behind the profound guilt that is in the mind. That is why you should not judge people for what they do. They are not doing anything against you. They are merely hiding behind their actions, and so are you. What you think people are doing to you is only your interpretation of what they are doing. What you think the body feels are only memories.

You see a world of pain, with no love. Humankind has some happy moments, a touch of heaven here and there, but then it finds suffering again. You think the world, or what you call 'life', is a roller coaster where you need to drop down in order to go up. You say that this is how life is: 'One needs to be in misery to be able to enjoy the goodness of life.' Why is that so? Would you like your son to suffer so he can enjoy the hugs that you give to him? A higher source does not know of suffering. It does not understand that its child suffers and why it suffers.

The ego cannot let you be in your true state of mind. If you find your true state of mind, you then find a higher source. The ego has washed its hands by making you believe that a higher source has given you a body that has all sorts of emotions and that gets sick and dies. There is no shifting of emotions in creation. Emotions only come from the body, but spirit is love. Sickness cannot come from love."

Chapter Seventeen

Antoine and Liliana are having dinner with some close friends. During the conversation, Antoine proclaims, "I will never die." Intrigued, Liliana leans into his ear and whispers, "So Antoine, you say you have reached immortality! I want it too. Tell me how." Antoine replies, "Dear, you are still thinking at the body level. Be patient."

"Everywhere you look you see death. Everything that seems to be alive dies so there is no life in what the world calls life. When men see death, they suffer. Men refer to the cause of their suffering due to the loss that they are accepting for those who are dying. In fact, the cause of suffering over death is the remembrance that all of humankind is to die, and dying is against reality. When men see birth, they rejoice. They remember creation and they remember it as innocently and purely as a newborn. To create is to bring into being. Being is to live. What lives does not die, so the time you assume as life is called existence.

Humankind produces children. It thinks it gives life, but that little body is just a continuation of the child's own ego-mind. The ego needs continuity to survive and the only way to survive is by keeping the continuity of the body. The ego keeps making new forms so long as men do not correct their minds and remember truth.

You think your children are your very own. No one and nothing belongs to you, but they belong to a higher source. The tree that gives fruit, the sea that brings fish, the sky where the birds fly; they are all part of your mind. They have a spirit and that spirit is love. Return to the creator what belongs to it, not in form, but in the spirit that abides in each form. Return by denying the form, by accepting and joining with the supreme mind of the world."

After the dinner, Antoine and Liliana go for a stroll. As they exit the restaurant, Antoine pauses. "Open your mind to understand," he says. "Because even our bodies are a memory."

Liliana's breath stopped. She did not know what to say or how to process what she had just heard. The statement shocked her and she had trouble controlling her emotions. Antoine noticed her paleness and her fidgeting hands.

"I know it is hard," he said. "The truth is very hard for the ego but one day you will understand. It all depends on you." Liliana did not respond right away. Not long after, she felt a sort of almighty presence, the most loving hug imaginable, embracing her.

"Anything that you can imagine belongs to you. It is in you, and still, you think that you have to get more. Humankind always wants more but it is never satisfied. For that reason, its existence revolves around seeking gratification.

Only the remembrance of a higher source can complete you. When you return to the creator what is its own, you have all. Not only are you returning what is in you, but you are returning yourself also, its beloved child. A higher source is waiting for your return. The creator wants its child to remember.

In the mind, you can only have by sharing what you want to have. There is no having without sharing. You cannot be generous with the world by sharing the illusion of death, for death is what you would then have. If you want life, you share life to have life. You cannot share life if you still share the concept of death, for death in itself is temporary. A higher source deserves to see its children in the realm of creation. It sees them through you when you are in your supreme mind and your supreme mind shares bliss and love with other minds. The thought of the ego is the thought of death, and a higher source knows of no death.

You are in a world of sacrifices. You are in a body that always wants something, but everything that it wants requires sacrifice. Even love, in your world, requires sacrifice. Sacrifice is to give up what you have for what you want. Do you think a higher source would have you sacrifice? If what you want is the abundance of the creator, you need not to sacrifice, for abundance is who you really are. Only in the dream do you sacrifice to get what you want.

The ego would have you sacrifice everything and anything, since what you ultimately want is love, and the ego has no love. There is no sacrifice that allows entrance into heaven. However, you must sacrifice death in order to live. Religious conviction claims that there is a hell and that men need to perform sacrifices to attain acceptance into heaven. Only heaven is real. Hell is just a thought of humankind.

If purgatory is where you atone for your sins, if such place is a place of temporary suffering and punishment then, isn't that place where you are and call life? The world of the ego is the world of misery and suffering. To go to heaven and not hell, you have to correct your mind from the ideas of hell to remember heaven, not in the future, for the future does not exist. It is in this present moment that you are in heaven and find a higher source that waits for the return of its sinless child.

Humankind has made up many beliefs. The mind is so confused that no one knows where to turn. Some people change their religion as they please. If they search for the spiritual, they run away from the world thinking the world of form is destructive. They isolate from it assuming that by not interacting with the world, their spirit will sustain serenity. Men yet fail to understand, that no matter how high up in the mountains they go, the world is still in them. To reach the spirit is to heal the world from the mind, even if bodies stand before the eyes.

Spirit is what you have always been. It is who you are. The body is an illusion of your dreams and to recognize your spirit, your mind must wake from the dream.

Spirit is the light in you. It is the one to lead you to your truth. Give your heart in honesty to your spirit and let it lead you through and teach you rightly. If the ego resists and begins to confuse you, release your inhibitions and let your guard down."

This is how miracles happen. Consider what the last paragraph means. To humble yourself about something, which you know nothing, about something you cannot see, is miraculous and satisfying. Nothing goes wrong there, absolutely nothing. Release yourself from everything on this earth to learn what humility is. Let your spirit do everything.

Give yourself to something and someone that you know you trust to make things right. Become vulnerable in a private place, alone.

"Tell your spirit that you do not know. Ask it to choose for you. If you can allow your spirit to choose for you, then humankind can also learn how to love. Love is what your spirit is. Without your spirit the mind cannot discern truth, therefore, death fills the void.

The ego-mind pretends to be with you and help you find the truth. It makes you believe that you have found enlightenment. How can a mind of perception experience illumination? How can anyone know the world when it is a world of questions? When there is knowledge, there are no questions left unanswered. Your spirit is like the light of the stars or the glimpse of the sunrise that wakes you gently.

Have faith in the truth and have the willingness to remember yourself. Be determined in the journey to the remembrance of your reality. The ego is shrewd and will lure you with its false impressions. You, who seem in love with the world and with the body, you think that you need to give up everything to join with your higher source. Not so. Remember, there are no sacrifices. Heaven and the world of form are two different worlds. One is real and the other is an illusion.

Your illusion is the world of pain, sickness and death. Your reality is the world of peace. If you want to remember the real world of immortality, renounce the world of death. To forsake one world in order to keep the other only means that you cannot have both worlds at once. They are opposites and they are both in your mind. You must leave the world that you do not want for the one you do want. Choose to keep the world that you love.

The body exists only for a period of time, a very short time - a flash in infinity. The ego gives you a time to exist without giving you a chance to choose for yourself. Now, it is up to you to choose if you want your existence to be controlled or you want to control how you want to exist. Since the mind makes the world that you are in, you choose either the world of light and peace or the world of sickness and insanity.

You can make the world of form into a beautiful paradise. You can be free of disease, hate, malice, evilness, suffering, tears, disappointments or torments if that is what you want. If you choose, you can be in love, in peace and joy with the whole world regardless of what the world seems to do. Both worlds of peace and misery are in your mind and it is up to you to choose which one you want to keep.

You have been aware of only one world, and you have thought that one day you will go to the world of heaven. You have known of separation, not union. You have known of pain and death, and you thought that you would never escape since you thought you were powerless. I tell you now that you have all the power to make of the world either a beautiful dream or a horrible nightmare. The ego-mind made you believe that you are nothing compared to the force of its will, when in fact, it was you who made the ego.

You do not need to do anything or go anywhere to attain what you already have. You do not need to keep what you do not want. You have the power that a higher source extended to you and you can play in paradise as your mind reigns in heaven. You are not at the mercy of the world. It does not matter how intimidating anything seems to be. You are at the mercy of your own self. What you feel is what you have chosen to keep.

Sometimes you have feelings that are out of control, that hurt and confuse you, and you shed tears. Feelings are thoughts; they are part of the body that responds to the mind. Feelings have no strength over you since they come from your own mind. If everything is in your mind, because you <u>are</u> a mind, how can anything have power over you, if even what you <u>think</u> has power, is really you?"

The mind is like a jewelry box where you keep your diamonds, pearls and whatever else you treasure most. That box stays in a safe-deposit box at the bank with lots of other boxes belonging to others. That is the analogy to the mind. Hold dear to that jewelry box. It is of value. No one can steal anything in it because no one can reach it. You own the box. It belongs to you.

Chapter Eighteen

*"**H**umankind has said the world is a dream. That statement is easily uttered but it is not easily understood. What that truly means is that the mind of the child of a higher source went into a deep sleep, and from that sleep the child began to dream.*

That dream became everything that you see, hear, touch and feel. You are the child of a higher source who fell asleep. Yes, the dream exists. It is tangible in time but it is not reality. The world of form is an illusion, full of sensory perceptions."

Antoine is a Real Estate Broker. He recently got a listing to sell a house in the desert in California. It was a beautiful home on the golf course with high, soaring ceilings, a private pool and a lush garden. Yes, in the desert! Imagine the maintenance! Since the owners lived in another state, they asked Antoine to stay in it for a few weeks. Liliana came along, taking the opportunity to write in a quiet, warm (actually hot) beautiful place. After the first week of being in the calmness and stillness of the desert, the voice tells Liliana, *"**You should interact with the world to heal from the dream, for to heal is to strengthen the mind.**"*

Liliana gets very excited because now she has a valid reason to go out and play. She thinks the message meant for her to go out to fancy restaurants, dancing, meeting people, etc. But, during their morning bike ride, as they ride further out into the village all they see is, well... desert!

Antoine: "This is the world that you see now and it is here for you to interact with it."

Liliana: "I never thought of it this way."

Antoine: "The dream is the dream. Your ego wants to limit you to certain categories instead of having you see all things the same."

"Everything in the world of form will perish, and what perishes has never been. Why remain attached to anything that perishes?

Where you are and what you call life is the dream state of your mind. In that state, your mind has identified itself with a body, which, with its functions, seems to be reality. The confidence on the body gives the world its seeming reality and certainly motivates the mind to invest its value on it.

You are in a world of perception and you make the world accountable for everything that you feel. When you feel anger or depression, you think that something that happened to you or that was done to you caused your feelings. What you feel is what you make out of the circumstances that appear as real to you.

Your reactions interpret events. No circumstances bring any feelings unless you judge the circumstances and accept the opinion of what you see. The feeling that your own judgment caused will last for as long as you want to keep the idea that the circumstances and the feelings are real.

The world stands on memories. What you project is what you have seen from before. In addition, since projection supports perception, you accept what you project. Who you believe you are is not your truth; it is your own memories."

Liliana shares with her mother her new relationship with Antoine, but she is still uncomfortable about mentioning the voice to her. Her family has noticed how Liliana has changed and they cannot comprehend how all of a sudden she is a writer. Liliana wants to bring her family up to date on her new spiritual breakthrough, but she stays on course and remains silent, reluctant to risk disapproval.

"Creation has no memories, but humankind does. Memories are of the past and the past is a delusion of time. Creation has only one thought and that is the thought of love. Love is in the present. The world is not responsible for

anything that you feel. The world does not make you sick nor does it make you suffer; the mind in fear does this. When you accept suffering, you believe in guilt and you do not want to see that the world is as guiltless as your spiritual mind.

You have seen cities that vanished, and wars where thousands and thousands of bodies died. You have seen catastrophes and plagues, and you might ask, 'How can all this be in my mind?' I assure you it is. Everything in the world is a mind and all you witness stays in your mind. However, nothing of what you have seen has happened from a sane mind.

The ego-mind wants to destroy, separate and kill. Even in the sorrowful and pitiful state that you notice in others, the ego-mind satisfies its goal of separating. Sorrow is of no joy and no love, and pain is one of the ego's goals.

Humanity is terrified of death and yet it values it. When you feel depressed and sick, and when you mourn for the ill or the dead, you accept death. Every moment you get angry or hold any resentment, you embrace death. The acceptance of any sensation or feeling is the acceptance of the dream, and the dream is death. What you accept is what is real to you, and that is how the ego controls you. It makes you see and feel all sorts of things for you to think the body is real. And if the body is real, then the ego is real.

Do not believe in humankind's behavior. No matter, judge it not and make it not real to you. The ego knows of separation and it cares for nothing. Even when the world gives a good moment, it is a dream. The illusion of goodness and love that the ego gives is by way of a trick."

A mother says she loves her daughter, but she can resent her for the damage of her dear body after giving birth to her, as well as the amounts of attention she steals from her. She gives her daughter kisses and pampers her, but then she shouts at her. She blames the child for depriving her of her freedom. She hides the guilt by caressing her body and tells her she loves her, showering her with gifts. Do not think the ego just has a face of malice. It is not only the horrors that we see. Everything that we see is of the mind.

The ego is non-stop structure, always building something. It does not rest. It gives us a sense of reality but it cannot afford to let us get wise to it. It gives us a landscaped garden and joy to thrive in its warm intentions. These are all senses, part of the body, and are unreal.

The ego-mind will do whatever it needs to do to keep us under its control. It gives us contentment in small doses so we do not run from its pain. It gives us the thought of joy and love for us to think that we are in reality.

"You do not have to stay in the dream of darkness. For centuries upon centuries, the world has been lost, and for all that it has done, it has always been disappointed. See the light that shines for your deliverance. See it in everyone in the world and they will see it in you. The light that shines on the world is the end of the illusion time, and time is death.

The release of the ego releases you to timelessness, and timelessness is freedom. By believing in time, distance and form, you believe that when you give something you then have it no more. In the ego, you can never be free. The body is limited to its form and functions and it has to follow the rules of the world.

Memories classify everything that you perceive. They give the meaning and value to the world of the ego. See with your eyes no more but with your heart. See yourself as one with the world to see who you really are. Reveal the truth of every person before the light of this moment now. The dream is the world of the ego, and that world is a world of chaos where everything is an illusion of judgments that you believe is your truth. Enjoy the silence of heaven and the certainty of a higher source.

The body is limited and it will never reach the capacity of expressing what the mind is. Free the mind to reach to the unlimited. Once you free your mind, you are free from the burden of pain and the fear that binds you to the insanity of the dream. Refute the body and free humankind. Release them from thoughts of guilt, for it is guilt that keeps the dream thriving.

A higher source is cause, and its children are its effect. Without a higher source there is no child, there is no life. A higher source being in you, the cause is also in you. When the mind-asleep made the ego, the ego turned the cause upside down. It projected the cause on the world of form. If the ego had left the cause in you, you would get rid of anything that is not of your truth.

You must always discard what is not of you. You have always thought that the cause is in the body or on something that is outside of you. However, when you see the cause outside of you, you are vulnerable to your own attack. Your attack is your own judgment and that judgment brings the meaning to what you see. You allow what you see to make you feel how you feel.

Would you not want to outsmart the ego? If you do, just remember to bring the cause back into your mind. After you understood that the cause is in you, would you still accept the cause of tears and grief?

There is no cause but a higher source and the effect of the cause shall be as the cause is. When you absorb this, all suffering is gone. To comprehend how the cause is in you, you must accept that the mind is one and *what appears to be external is in you. You have the power to choose the cause of every moment of your existence.*

Trust my voice. I share with you truth. There is no need to trust the world anymore. It has given you no response; it has shown you no truth. Think of the one thing that has been unfailingly certain. You have heard of many seeming truths, and each one is different from the other. Truth is one.

The world has given you no peace of mind, not at all. It has made you think that peace is not in you and that you can only find peace by doing what distracts you from it. You can argue what you want and shut your ears to hear nothing. Yet, if you look into your heart, if you close your eyes and quiet your mind, you hear the voice of truth. The quest for love and truth will last forever if you continue to put your faith where there is no truth at all. If you do not believe in what has given you no truth, if you do not want to believe in anything anymore, at least go to your heart. Your heart will never lie to you. Your heart is your true self.

The child of a higher source who sleeps and dreams of nightmares deserves to wake and to see itself in the light of its home where there are no false impressions. Why, when you have all, would you choose to suffer? Why when there is light, would you choose to stay in darkness?

You not need be in the world of illusive ideas. You, who want peace, ask yourself, why not stop doing everything that disturbs your peace and keeps you from finding it? The light has come and the voices of heaven whisper in you to accept your supreme mind. Heaven is close, so close to you. There is nowhere for you to go.

In the dream, the mind lives in fear and it suffers in guilt. Why think the world is for you to suffer? It is difficult to deem the body as un-reality. The body is tangible. You see it, you feel it and you sense it. However, if you have the power to make yourself believe that the body and the world of form are real, you can also have the power to believe that it is all a dream.

How would you not believe the world is outside of you? You reach out to something because it is out there. You say you feel alive, but once your body is gone, what is left? Where do your ideas go? When the ego made the body, it made sure that in time and distance you would never think that you are a mind.

The body is there but it is not your reality. Reality is everlasting and what is perishable cannot be who you are in truth. Humankind's mind made the dream and it guides the dream as well. Its convictions of its existence ground its concerns to preserve itself.

The world invests in the body to maintain a seemingly healthy life. How can you keep the body from

197

sickness and death when you dwell in the mind that knows nothing of life? Instead of investing on the mortal ideas of the ego-mind, invest in redirecting your mind.

Ask your spirit to restore your being, enter the light and purity of your real mind, which transcends throughout you. Dreams are temporary ideas and the dream will never cease to be the dream. It is real only if the mind believes that it is real."

Chapter Nineteen

The world of a writer can be as quiet as a falling leaf or as loud as thunder. Liliana is not completely isolated from the world but she spends a greater part of her days at home where she works and often shares dinner with friends. Antoine, on the other hand, is rather all over his world. Everyday he has a new agenda and he easily goes along with whatever needs to be done. His phone rings, his clients come. From the moment he wakes-up, he is on the go. But no matter what he does, when Liliana writes, a profound silence occupies their two-story home. The presence of the voice is so powerful that nothing can disturb its continuous flow. Even when Liliana gets up to "shake it off" or to take care of things around the house, when she gets back to her desk the voice resumes its message exactly where it paused.

"To the world, the higher source is awe-inspiring. Only the extraordinary and the pretentious are of this caliber. This is why the ego-mind plays and pretends to be a higher source. If you sense amazement in the thought of a higher source, then you are saying that you are not of yourself. A higher source does not separate its child from

itself. It is as the child and with the child, and love consumes both.

The ego wants to reinforce the thought that a higher source's omnipotence is over you; that you suffer at its mercy. A higher source's will is its child's will. It is your will, and all there is for the child to give to his creator is gratitude. If you feel amazement in the thought of a higher source, exchange the thoughts from the dream for the love of your creator and give it your thankful heart. Thankfulness, love and acceptance: This is respect. What you respect is who you are.

If you accept the ego it is because you respect it. You then neglect a higher source. If you have respect for the ego, you have no respect for a higher source. If you respect a higher source, you have nothing to do with the ego. In the rules of the dream, if you respect, you demonstrate it by what you do, not by what you say. Your actions reflect your respect regardless of what your words say. If you respect a higher source, you show it your respect with what it knows, and it knows nothing of the dream. A higher source knows of love and sharing and so, you show your respect by sharing love in the supreme mind of everyone in the world.

Your actions express gratitude. You give and show thankfulness to the person that has shown you love. You show thankfulness toward a creator by being with it, as a creator loves to be with its child. Thankfulness and respect is all there is for a creator.

In your world of differences, you constantly waver between your choices. What you choose is what is important to you. Therefore, if you choose the dream, it means illusions are important to you. To understand yourself and the dream you must observe what you see. Your actions show who you are and what you love. If you love a creator and accept that you are creation, you choose your spirit to translate your gratitude and respect toward a creator."

To show that you embrace love, unite with the world in forgiveness. You have a gift of free will. No one can tell you how to use it. You must decide for yourself even if you think you allowed someone else to decide for you. Would you allow another's ego to dominate you if you remember that you both share the same mind? It is always your choice: to subsist in the ego or to respect a higher source.

"The ego plays the part of a higher source and wants you to bow to it. It wants you to think of itself as supreme. By feeling amazement for its ideas, you think of yourself as insignificant. The thought of a higher source scares humankind because humanity is limited by its mind's fear.

In truth, you find yourself one with a higher source. Furthermore, since the sum of truth gives you no illusions or senses, there is no amazement to feel. A higher source should not scare you. Why would you be scared of your creator when you are its extension of love? Why believe that you remain estranged from a higher source if it is one with you? Why not acknowledge truth, if in heaven, you are freedom itself?

The ever-shifting dreams from humankind are in its dream state of mind. What effects could the dreams of the children have when they wake next to their creator? Nothing can possibly change what the child means to a higher source; creation means all and it will never change. When you forgive, you forgive not the sin of those you think are in sin. If you see sin, you believe in sin. Believing in sin is denying truth. Forgive the thought of humankind, of its own ego and the thought of its ego in you. Accept every person as the sinless child that they are. Accept the world as your kin, for reality is in them as well as it is in you. The creator is in everything that you set your eyes on. It is everywhere you are. A creator is not in the heaven that is above you. Nothing is above you. Everything is within you. The creator is in the heaven of your mind.

Think and see how many ideas separate you from creation. Think of the worries and concerns that keep your thoughts from the thought of the creator. Think of the time of your existence. Why would a creator have you suffer in a limited body so that when it dies you join with it? Why would a higher source do that to its own child? When you understand that the dream is the illusion of your mind, would you accept suffering? Would you hold on to pain? If you are the child of the creator, why are you not with your creator?

The child has been lost in the forest. It has been trying to get home, but it does not know how. Your creator is waiting for your return. It knows that you have heard the truth. It knows that its child has heard the word of his spirit to guide him back to his reality. Creation lives infinitely and it resides in the same place even after you decide to return. You have the power that your creator extended to you where death is not an option.

Walk into the realm of creation and see yourself in the mirrors with the angels. See your likeness and know that heaven is where you belong. The doors have always been open, and now is when you enter through them. Go there and live-forever. Death is not real.

Death is an illusion. The body is what dies, and the body is an illusion of the mind of the child of heaven. The mind lives and spirit always shines in its entirety. Accept truth and be forever invulnerable.

What you think you know is of no consequence. Humankind can tell you many things about reality. Yet, what does the ego know? When you accept reality, you will understand that all the things the dream has given you have been figments of your imagination.

There is something to understand about the ego. It needs your investment in its world. The ego enforces its appearance so that you cease to remember you are spirit abiding in the realm of creation. When you identify with creation, you seize the influence from the ego and you enforce its ideas no more. Perhaps you have found the happiness of a higher source; but in a world of scarcity, you will never find what it does not have. The ego made the body for your perception to look for what you want where you will not find it.

The journey to heaven will be long, but only if you choose the ego-mind. If you accept the world that the ego has given you, you will exist in imaginary thoughts of sin, pain and death. You will go around in circles searching to fulfill the void in your heart. You will believe in illusions until the day that you get tired of pain and suffering. You will then beg for no more misery and you will ask for the remembrance of the ultimate truth of your existence.

If you still think that a higher source is far from you, the journey back home will be impossible. You can never find your truth until you go within. The creator and the world are in your mind.

Will a creator speak to you? A creator only knows the language of love. If you speak to a higher source, it will only understand what is in your heart, the heart of your mind. Your perceptive mind cannot understand how to communicate with a higher source. Your spirit, who knows your heart, will translate all to your creator and it will respond with its love. The body knows of voices and words; the mind communicates with its soul. Communication is continuous and the mind that discriminates cannot communicate."

With her family still in New York City, every day Liliana calls to talk to them. As she cares for them, they care for her. She grew up with caring, tenderness and affection, so when she remembers her moments of love and she sees people expressing love, she questions, "If everything in the world of form is the ego and the ego has no love, that means there is no love in this world; what then are the moments of love? What are those years of joy that I shared with my brother as I grew up? What are those moments that tickle us and make us giggle? Parents adore their children and couples get lost in each other's words. What does it all mean?"

"A mind that thinks in time is already breaking the continuous thread of communication. It uses the body to express its ideas from the past. It uses the body, not to

communicate, but to attack since the body's behavior is a response to the meaning of what the mind has seen. In your acceptance of spirit and love, your supreme mind gives you the understanding of your truth. That is how you communicate with the world when you join with their supreme mind and see your kin not in their ego-mind.

Your spirit teaches you the right way to communicate. It translates your message of love and forgiveness. Give up words, sounds and gestures. They are inadequate, and limited.

Words, sounds, and gestures limit the power of your mind. They express nothing because they are parts of form. When you try to convey a message, what you say and what you do will only be a translation of what the other sees and hears. That is why the world is in confusion. An oracle will always see the self that bears its fears and guilt. While you ignore that you are a mind, nothing of what you want to say will convey. Only when you communicate with the mind will your message get through. Ask your spirit to teach you communication. Let it bring your message of love and peace to the world.

Your spirit knows all that is good for you. It will teach you and it will teach those around you what is of love. Your spirit will give you the answer to everything that you question. With its light, it shines on everything and lets you see what everything really is. You have faith in miracles, you have seen them and you wish for them again.

A miracle is an expression of your spirit. It is a reflection of its presence in the presence of your faith. If you put your faith in your spirit, your dream will be a miraculous journey. The enemy will turn to friend; the sick will heal; the lost will be found; the problems will be resolved; the questioning will be answered and the thirst for knowledge will be satisfied. Miracles are an expression of truth, a manifestation of love. Invite your spirit into your mind and you will see the light of supreme love around you. When you share your purity with all, your world becomes a pure world.

If you ask your spirit for merely the things that pleasure you, you then single out that weakness, and the ego will lead. You do not want to make part of the dream holy and part of it ego.

If you pretend to share bliss with a person just because you are fond of him, and then deprive another person from bliss because he is not of your liking, you are not sharing. Sharing is not separating or judging. All of humankind needs blessings. The 'all' cannot be all without all. The ego is not to decide for a higher source. All your kin are like you and you are to share the love of truth with them. You cannot keep bliss for yourself.

How can you separate from what is in your mind and how can you judge what is in your mind? When you judge, you are judging yourself. When you heal, you are healing yourself. If you individualize, you are splitting from the whole, and without all, healing cannot be complete. Once you accept wholeness in your mind and you are willing to join with all, regardless the judgments against anything or anyone, then you are ready to heal.

Only your spirit can heal. If you let the ego choose for you, it will choose what hurts you most. The ego knows what makes the heart cry and it knows the exact time to give it to you. People have happy events but no one is ever truly happy and in peace. That is how 'life' is, as humankind says it. Humankind, in most times, believes that there is always something to work through; it has been convinced that happiness does not exist, not always. In its world, possibly, this is true. Why would a world provide for something it does not know of?

Happiness does exist.

The ego is the mind in darkness. That is why you cannot see what you cannot see. When you criticize, you are judging without knowing. Not knowing leads to assuming. The ego-mind assumes, it does not know. It makes its world believe it has knowledge, but humankind only sees what the ego-mind decides to see. The world that you see and that you have is the world that you wish for.

Now you question, 'Why do I feel pain if that is not what I wish?' You are in your ego and the mind wants that pain. Pain is the projection of guilt in the ego-mind.

Every person of the world is guiltless and harmless. It is you, when you look at him or her, who projects your own judgment onto every other person. You bring the past to the moment and from those memories, you judge every action that everyone in the world makes. You give your own definition to what everyone says and what everyone does. You assume what people think. If you correct your perception, there will be no assumptions. You will see who everyone really is and you will know what they think for their mind is one with yours. Leave judgment aside and accept the world as part of you, as one with you.

In the world of form, there is space, distance and categorization. That is exactly how the ego made it, for you to see the world as apart from you. Certain that the ego would do anything to keep everything separate, the ego made the body with eyes to see so that you would visualize what you think even when you do not understand it.

Perception or observing is not knowledge; you imply your own discrimination. When you close your eyes, where is the world? When your eyes are open, the objects are out there. Even so, when the eyes are closed, everything you have seen afar is within you. Everything that you see is in your mind. Given that, everything has a mind; you are one with every mind. It is then your choice to be in your mind-asleep which limits you to fear, or to be one with the supreme mind, which extends its love.

When you see any person, you are seeing yourself. Selfishness is of the ego since it thinks only of itself and for itself. As long as you associate with the ego, you disassociate from everything else. Nothing is only yours. What you have is in your mind, and you share it with the whole world. It is when you let the ego dictate your life that you think in form and you follow the idea that what you have is where you are. What you possess is only what you think belongs to you. Selfishness is egoism, self-centered, not of others. Altruism is that which is concerned with all others, and is real."

Chapter Twenty

Antoine lives his life with ease and certainty. He works hard and he is very professional, yet he does not drown himself in a sea of worries. Somehow, and no one knows how, he has time for everything and everyone. And how he gets everything done – on time – is a mystery! Liliana desires his energetic and easygoing pace but she constantly worries and gets anxious, and she is in a constant battle with time.

Antoine: "Why would you worry about tomorrow if tomorrow is not here?"

Liliana: "So you mean to just sit around and let tomorrow come?"

Antoine: "No. You are power and I know that you are power, but I also know that you still do not recognize it. You need to use your spirit as your guide. Give your day to your spirit with complete faith and everything will be taken care of."

"Correction is acknowledging your truth. It is reawaking in heaven. It is the remembrance of you. You are asleep in dreams of death, and that is why deliverance

starts from the self and is of the self. You are in a world of senses and what you see is a passing fantasy that leaves nothing. The more you understand, the more you remember what you already know.

When you share holiness with the mind, you share deliverance with the world. With your spirit, you remind people's minds of the light that is already in them. It will ultimately be everyone's decision to accept truth, as it is your decision to accept your light and accept the holiness of reality.

When you teach anyone in the world, you should not teach what is right or what is wrong. In timelessness there is no right or wrong, there is only one reality, and that is what you want to share. Your spirit does not argue, it does not impose and does not attack. To say to anyone that you are right or that he is wrong is an attack. Your spirit does not know right or wrong, it only teaches love. If a person argues, let him argue, since what he is arguing about is not his reality. Whoever is in his right mind does not need to be defended.

The body that you see that is not of your reality has yet a time to exist. During its existence, it does not matter what it does. However, that does not mean you can go on carelessly in the world. Some people may take the dream as if they are now free and they can do whatever they please. If you believe in what the ego says, you would only give it more power to keep you captive in its games of sorrow. Freedom is of the mind not of the body.

Use the body to teach love and peace of the heart, which teaches forgiveness. As you start nurturing your mind and understanding your awareness, you should not decide how to teach love on your own, otherwise you would be doing what you have learned from the ego-mind.

The monuments the world has built may seem magnificent, but they are incomparable to your supreme mind. In reference to 'form', monuments are limited and they perish. The ego is not perfect. You think diversity is what makes the world perfect, and yet you are in search of perfection. In the perceptive mind, you desire perfection. You then compare what you have with what you want.

In comparison, you are seeking something better. By looking for something better, you are looking for your reality since all that is from a higher source is perfect; and what is perfect does not need comparison. What you love you may think is perfect. Nevertheless, in the world you cannot find anything perfect even when you make yourself believe that something is perfect, for your body is imperfect. You compare your body with another body and you find things that you would rather change. The world thinks that it is vanity to love your own body and you feel shameful about it.

The ego-mind made your body. Since the ego-mind is part of your mind then you made your body just as it is; with every defect you contemplate. The higher source did not make your body. It was not your parents.

If you want to see perfection, look for a higher source in all that you see. You will see everything shine in purity, as the sparkle of the finest diamonds. You will see the colors of heaven transcend into one another through every form. You will see humankind with an angelic glow that emits the purity of the child in them. You will spot no flaw in anything that you see.

Turn your eyes away from the dream. The ego has blinded you until this moment. See the past no more. Release the memories and be free to see the present. The present is where you are and where perfection is complete.

Actions and repetitive patterns come from the memories that you have accumulated throughout the existence of the dream state of mind. Those memories judge everything where you are so you always miss the reality of your circumstances. What you see and what you want from what you see is the same as the memory that is judging for you. Let go of past thoughts."

If we could throw away our painful thoughts the way that Liliana throws away clutter, this book will be easier to understand. Antoine laughs. During one of those frantic clean-ups, Liliana finds her books on "shamanism" and all the "isms" she has investigated. She shows Antoine and muses about how none of it ever made any sense to her.

Antoine: "How were you supposed to find your sense of being if you run away from the world? When you go to a place of worship you might feel peaceful, but that is only because you are hiding. What happens when you have to deal with the world? It is from the world that you have to heal and it is in the world where you find your 'self'."

"Do not give the ego what it wants. Give yourself what you deserve. The more you dwell in the past, the more you let the ego lead. Your spirit will think for you if you let it. Let the angels come to take your hand and show you how to open your wings and fly in the skies of life. Let the angels restore the freedom in you and the innocence of all. Fly with the angels to where your creator is, and play with the rainbows of grace that are all over heaven.

Leave the world of mortality where everything falls into rottenness. Leave the lies, the fears and the incertitude. What have they brought to you but doubt?

Stop feeling guilty for what is not real. Return home. There is no need to be lost anymore. Enter into the timelessness and leave behind the memories of destruction and death. You are in a world that is not your reality. What you see with the eyes is not truth. What you feel is not who you are. A higher source created its children to be forever joyful. It would be insane to accept a world of suffering and death when you know that you can be with your creator and share its love in infinity.

Truth is simple: You are light. Who you believe you are in body is a mind lost in darkness, which after all, is from the dream.

The ego-mind uses its defense mechanisms to protect itself, because it knows that it is weak. Only with your power can the ego exist. It knows that if it lets its guard down, it will be gone. He who is powerful does not need to protect himself from anything. Power is power and nothing can weaken power. Power stands on its own and does not need to do anything. Humankind is relentlessly surviving. When you come to life and see with your mind what you have made, and how untrue the ego is, you will laugh at it. You will laugh at how needless are the tears that you have shed.

The truth is still hard to comprehend when the body and the world appear as real. Until you understand that you are a mind, you will not be able to see the difference between what is real and what you choose to believe is real. Your mind is power and you have chosen the mind that made the world that you consider as real.

You can use that power for what you want, to fail in the world of false impressions or to reign in reality. Your *power is a creator's power and until you recognize that, you will not remember reality.*

You do not need to go against the ego. To fight the ego is to side with it and if you side with it, you make it real. You then lose your power. Simply let it go. Free yourself from it.

Why would you invest in something that is ephemeral and that will never bring you peace and love? Why would you distance yourself furthermore from what is your nature and what is your truth? You are dreaming and that dream has turned against you. Why do you continue to rely in fantasies?

Fantasies are imaginary thoughts to be amused by. However, the moment they start turning ugly, you can stop fantasizing. You are a mind. You are thinking everything that you consider as real. Why keep painful and fearful thoughts? Why keep in the mind what disrupts your peace? The ego is an idea and you are keeping that idea.

What you witness is an idea. What you foresee are wishes and what you feel are memories. Think in the mind level to understand what is real. The desires of the body are the ego's plan for you to remain true to its design. As you desire, you want and you wish to get. Thus, you think you will find satisfaction by getting what you wish. Everything that the body demands are wishes from the mind-asleep to reassure its ideas of form. The body is your thoughts. It takes the shape of your thoughts. No eyes of the world are shining and sparkling pure. The eyes of the world are eyes that shed tears and that show a mind lost in darkness.

Eyes that cry cannot be eyes of love. The light-mind, the mind of love, will not let itself be broken. Open the door to your soul and let the truth shine through your eyes. Your eyes will show the brilliance of your heart and the purity of your mind. In the ego, your eyes never shine. They show the pain and darkness of the ego-mind. When you look into a person's eyes, heal the darkness of his ego-mind. Let the light of your spirit shine in both of your eyes. Become one with the light-mind of this person and let him see his light in you. Your mind of truth is luminous, powerful and pure as the stars. If you renounce the ego and accept the spirit in you, the light in you will illuminate the world.

The investment that you put in the body not to make it sick or old will only make it sicker and older because that investment comes from fear and not love. The ego will not let the body shine from the truth in you. It keeps the body dull with thoughts of hate and sadness and it brings its own destruction by what will hurt the body the most.

It is not what you do to the body that makes it radiant; it is the light of the mind, which glows throughout the body. In the memories of the mind is where you find the identity in which the body gets its name. That identity in which you are male, female, young, old, small, big, whatever you believe that you are. That identity, which is of the ego-mind, vanishes when your awareness is in your spirit's light."

*****

"Presence is timeless. Therefore, when you are now, there is no ego. When there is no ego, there are no past memories to linger on. Presence is a state of mind. In presence, there are no senses but the total awareness of timelessness. Bring your awareness to this moment to realize that everything that you have experienced is just an illusion of time. In this moment, you are a holy child and not the little identity of the ego that gets old and dies. Let this moment take you to your supremacy. Share this moment with the world and join with it in creation to reunite with a higher source.

Memories make up the responses to the world and they shape each personality. That personality is the reaction that each one lays upon everything that he or she sees. Each reaction accords to the meaning that the mind gives to the world. Your personality is how you choose to project your fears upon the guilt of the separation. Each personality is different from the other regardless of the circumstances that they share.

After the separation, the boundlessness of the mind disintegrated into millions of other ego-minds. That is why every mind is different. Nevertheless, no matter how each personality is classified, it is from the mind-asleep and not from truth. A higher source did not raise its children differently nor did it give to one more than to the other. The creator extended its totality to its child all the same, equally, in unity. The personality that you identify with is the ego that you made. Even the innocent and good aspects of your personality are of the ego.

Every trait that you assume as part of yourself separates you more from reality. You have only one inheritance and that is the will of a creator. The will of a higher source is what you own. The rest is an invention by a stranger that pretends to be your friend and pretends to love you but has given you nothing of what you ever needed.

That stranger comes with gifts, but only to steal away your inheritance. Would you let anyone steal the wealth that your creator willed for you? Would you let a stranger hypnotize you and give you no worth? If you value what you have, you will not let it go. How much do you value the creator? How much do you value peace? Only in reality do you find peace, the total peace of mind.

There is no total peace in the dream. You are the peace that you are looking for. Everything that you do or that you accept from the dream is designed to get rid of peace. Look at how it has been. Look at everything that you do. Do not blame others. Truthfully ask, why do you do what you do? What is your motivation? What is your drive?

Your mind confuses you with the answers. By confusing you, it does not let you figure anything out. Ask honestly, and if it is peace and love that you desire to have, then ask if it is still of any worth to continue what you are doing or what you were going to do. You think what you are doing today is for the peace of tomorrow. Tomorrow is not now. What makes you think that tomorrow you will not desire something different? Only by being in the present, and looking within will you find certainty, and therefore peace.

You are in a world in which you have to do, produce, consume and grow. You are in a world of competition. You compete for something that only you think is of worth, and you are willing to do whatever it takes to achieve and win what you compete for. Do not give the wealth of your peace away for something that brings you nothing. Follow the world of motion for as long as the body exists; but instead of doing what you need to do with fear and scarcity, do <u>with</u> the love of a higher source.

Your creator does not want you to sell your peace, or to work and struggle for its love. It wants you to share its will with your kin in the world. For spirit, there is no doing. For the ego, there is no stillness. When you are in turmoil, do not dwell on what you need to do. Instead, quiet your mind, take your hands away from the turmoil and let your spirit give you the answer of all and guide you on your path.

Nothing matters in the world of form. In the end, everything disintegrates to dust. Everything that you adopt as significant will become insignificant. What matters is what is important. If a creator is important to you, then nothing of the dream should matter. The 'id' feigns that a higher source matters. Really, what matters to the ego-mind is its illusions.

Whether it is something that is for you or something that is of you, you put your worries onto what is important to you. You give importance to what you value in your limited world; otherwise, you would not be accepting the thoughts that bring suffering. What matters to you is what you think matters, because if what matters to you does not matter to another man, then does it really matter? You are the one to decide what matters. The dream will matter to you for as long as you keep the promise of the separation from creation.

If you are fascinated with the world of form; if you still see it as a wonderful place that is filled with pleasurable gifts, your mind is accepting fantasies, and you would rather take the pain and the misery that comes from underneath the gifts. If you prefer the world of limitations, you are still afraid of your own power. If you accept the ego, you let guilt and fear dominate you; you would rather be enslaved in the mills than be a king in heaven."

If you were onstage in a play, you might not be able to play two characters in the same scene, one part as slave and the other as king. However, once you have the crown on your head, you will not want to take it off and scrub the floor with chains around you. The mills and heaven are both in your mind. The slave and the king are both in your mind.

Chapter Twenty-One

The fresh breeze, the warm sun in the clear sky and the blooming trees frame the California mornings. After their coffee, Antoine and Liliana start their day with a run. On one of those beautiful mornings, Antoine notices a coin on the ground. It shines as calmly as the blue sea. He picks it up and hands it to Liliana.

Antoine: "When I find something, I bless the person who lost it."

Liliana: "I never thought of it that way. So, it is not just at night, or in the morning, or when I write that I should correct my mind and accept my reality?"

Antoine: "Every moment is for us to think of all, and to join in the mind. When I see those beautiful hills, I think of everyone living in every gorgeous house and I bless them because they are in me, and I want us all to be together in our reality."

"You are blessed and that blessing is part of you. Bless now the world, bless everything that you hold and touch and that you see. Bless as you accept the purity of the world.

The ego-mind makes you think the world is evil, full of wrongdoing and limitations. It chains everyone in his or her own skin, yet everyone in the world is the child of a creator and is integrated. In the ego-mind you are one, and you will be like this no matter how long your mind sleeps. The world of the ego is a place of instability, uncertainties and scarcity. It is a world of private minds, and each mind has an identity to defend. That world will never have a place in the realm of a higher source.

When men are in their private world, they are constantly guarded and they regard the world as an enemy to them. They believe they need to protect themselves and so they attack as they defend what they adopt as theirs. They defend their dignity, their values and their integrity. Nevertheless, they are just defending themselves from their 'self.' They defend their 'id' from the world of the ego itself. The child of a higher source has nothing to defend and nothing to lose. Humankind has limitations in its mind. In its world, it has to defend itself in order to prevail.

When anyone attacks you; they attack themselves; we are one. If any persons insults you; they are insulting themselves; we are one. What anyone says about you; they say of themselves; we are one. An odd self-motivation of the ego is that it makes you feel you have to defend yourself. There is nothing to defend. When you are within your supreme mind, you see, what you defend means nothing, and what you attack is the same as what you defend, which means nothing.

When you make the body real, you assail the truth. When you join with the mind and become one with those in the world, the attack will cease to be an attack and become a blessing.

If there is nothing to attack, there is nothing to defend. You choose. The more you defend yourself, the more you attack. The act of attacking gives power to the ego. Do you still want the ego? Do you still believe it? Do you still think it is real to you? If you want to maintain the conviction that the 'id' is who you are, you are saying that you are not the child of a higher source. Who are you then? Where is your source? What is your truth? Is it pain and death? Why choose the same all over? If you still think the world of finite forms is your reality you still value what it gives to you, including misery.

You will remain loyal to the dream for as long as you are afraid to remember reality and recognize the higher source. However, sometimes you reach a point where you've had enough with so much suffering in the world. It is then when you feel you have the right to live. Living is of your truth. You would not find yourself until you gave up the idea of your 'id' and the tremulous occurrences of the world.

If you agree to lies, you still feel the need to protect the private world with which you identify. Lies only exist in the mind that values them. When you lie to someone, you lie to yourself. The liar is in the mind of the person he is lying to. The mind of the person lying is one with the other. If you think that people can lie to you, you believe that you can single out by seeing only the limited body and you do not take yourself genuinely. Remember that mind reads mind, but you can only understand that when you accept that you are a mind. There are no lies. Lies are of the dream, and since it is unreal, lies then should be insignificant.

When you separate from the whole, you diminish your power completely. And, you who fight and destroy in search of power, why would you want to give your power up? Be who you are, a mind, a supreme mind, and be your own power. You do not know how blessed you are. You will find completion when you join with your spirit. In your supreme mind you will become one with your power.

Only in the mind-asleep will you conceive of yourself as limited and incomplete. That mind makes you see yourself in a body that is always aching and burdened by its own needs. When you try to hide something, what you are trying to hide is your own fear and nothing else. You hide your thoughts assuming no one will know them, but be sure that the whole world knows your fear, for they are also in fear. No one realizes this while their awareness is in the body. Feelings and pain in the body are the reflection of fear.

Everything that you do to the body is an act of punishment. Nevertheless, all the attraction to the body is the reflection of the fear and the guilt after the separation. The mind is punishing itself for its own guilt. If there is no guilt then there is no body.

The child of a higher source is guiltless and it shares its purity with creation. You are free of guilt, as your creator created you guiltless. The guilt is only of the dream. When the holy child wakes, his mind wakes from fear and guilt. The memories of fears will be gone; the dream will be gone and creator and child will be as they always have been.

A higher source and your spirit communicate by "being" and with love. If you pray for love, love of the mind, a higher source will respond. If you want just a body for love, which means you choose the scarcity of the mind-asleep, you still hold the idea of completion with another body. If you just want one body to love, you are saying that you do not love the world in sameness. If you do not love the world, you do not love a higher source. Therefore, if you love, you love all. You have to share love in the mind first for the body to learn how to love.

The love that the body responds to is not love; it is the fancies of love. How can that love be real when it only exists while you contemplate its idea with the body? In the dream, love is perception, and later it dies. The reality of love abides in the infinite.

When you give something to someone, you know you have given it and you know that person has received it. If you share love with someone you do not need to prove that you love. There is nothing to prove.

Why do you need to promise to be faithful in your loving if you truly love? Why would you need to keep giving what is already one? Love is not an object; it is not a thing. It is not something that you can give and then take back. Love is mutual, not given, because only the body gives. Love is of the heart, and what is of the heart shares.

When you love, you love forever. Humankind thinks it can choose what to love, how little, how much and for how long. The search for love in the body is endless and painful. The body is an empty shell. It cannot offer infinite love. The body is mortal and the mind is immortal.

Everything people do, they do because they are seeking love. Wherever you look and whatever you see, is asking for love. Everywhere you look, you find a chance for you to share love, and as you share love, you see it bloom in you. Do not lose any opportunities to share the love of your heart. Even those who you think are at war with you, they are asking for love. Fill them with love, for your love will only make you stronger. A full heart is solid and cannot be broken.

Imagine an enemy attacking you. First, realize, whatever he is doing, he is not doing it to you but to himself. His actions are simply coming out of his insecurities. He is projecting his own guilt and he is missing love. You do nothing in response to what he is doing to you. However, with your mind, you remind him of love. His heart will then complete and his ego will bow in gratitude.

Love conquers all. Love discloses your look at truth, shining in everything. You are love, and it has power over everything in the world. You will heal the sick, you will heal yourself, and you will be at peace. You have found love now, and now is forever. Keep your love. Keep what is yours and cherish it. Keep yourself alive by embracing love and sharing love with the world. If you turn to the dream, you will not see love. What you will see is what you long to see. The heart of the child of a higher source is love, where your love lives in purity, and where all of you are kindness."

Chapter Twenty-Two

Social events remain a part of Antoine and Liliana's world. As they are getting ready to go to a celebration, Antoine notices that Liliana changes one dress after the other. She gets frustrated, angry, upset . . . she cannot get dressed.

Liliana: "Look at this body, it's huge! How can this be happening when I'm not eating any more that what I usually do? Nothing fits! I'm like a balloon!"

Antoine: "The ego is keeping you busy with the body. By bloating it, you become worried and you perceive your world with anxiety. Also, the thought of existing becomes real, like getting dressed, eating, losing weight. Your thoughts get lost and you lose connection with your higher source."

Liliana: "So, should I just let my body bloat until it explodes?"

Antoine: "Reverse the idea of bloating and choose the kind of body that you want."

"There is no waiting and no doing to find a higher source. The creator is in you. You have believed that you

are something the ego has wanted you to think you are. The body and the identity that you are part of is an illusion of the child of a higher source in you. It is a belief in an inspiration that you made when you decided to split from your source.

Accepting reality is humbling. It is seeing your reflection on everything and everyone in the world regardless of what the world wants you to see.

The ego is arrogant; it makes you think that it is everything. It makes you see a world of variation for you to compare yourself and justify your actions, which is the manifestation of the attack of your own guilt. It presumes it has love but on the contrary, it has no love."

Liliana: "One thing that I have noticed since I started writing and communicating with the voice is that I no longer feel the need or the desire to feel accepted by the world. I no longer fantasize of luxuries, fame and proving my talent and creativity to others. It feels good to be released of such a burden, especially when my desires depended primarily on my looks. Looks change and wane."

"Those who embrace their reality and walk with love are not of self-importance because they share their self with everything in their world. They extend their purity to

the world, and when they join with the reality of all, they restore their power within themselves.

Do not allow deceit. The power that you have is to bring love to this world of darkness and deficiency. Your power is to live in overall peace, joy and love with the world, regardless of the misery that the ego wants to impose.

You are as a higher source created you. You, who love to play, and want to play, do not play in a world to destroy and be destroyed; rather, play in a world of peace and love. The dream of pain will be over when you find no more tears to shed. The dream will end when your mind chooses to dream no more. When the mind invests in the dream, it ignores reality and relies on deceptions.

Share truth with the world. Would you leave those you love alone in a world of suffering? Would you take them with you to where they live forever? Would you not shine your spirit on them for their mind to be enlightened? The safety of heaven is with everyone. Heaven will protect you even if you are lost in the woods, with crows and wolves howling at you. Those who are to attack you will bend to the power of heaven abiding in you."

Antoine asks Liliana to tell him a certain story about her life. He has asked before and he always requests the same story. Liliana asks him why he keeps asking her to repeat that particular story. He tells her that it is a vehicle for healing. Liliana somewhat reluctantly tells him the story one more time. She admits to herself that she wants to be released from a vague but persistent feeling of guilt. She does notice that the first few times she told him the story, it was filled with details and emotions. Now, after several times of repeating it, healing has occurred and she can hardly remember the same details, and she notices a great detachment from almost every aspect of the story.

"The ego gives no safety. You can run from the rain but the water will always get you wet. You insure everything that you have in the world of form, but when a fire starts, it burns everything that you own. You may replace what you had, but never get back what you adored. You plan, you save for the future, but you never know when the mind in fear will retaliate with the body and leave you in agony.

Nothing made of illusions can bring you safety. You can hide all you want and protect yourself, but you will never be safe. The ego never protects you from anything that it gives. Its purpose is to steal what you have. Why would you hire a thief to watch your home while you were away? A man thinks that at home he is safe from the dangers of the world. He cannot see that even in the most secure places he will never be safe from the sorrows of his heart and the sickness of his body.

Only in heaven will you find freedom.

The world will know of safety when it knows heaven is the real home, since nowhere in the world can one feel at home. People try to make a home from an empty space where they exist and they fill it with ornaments that represent their 'id'. They devote their thoughts on how to make it the best of everything, but then they abandon it in search for a better one. People move from land to land - from cities to countries. People move in search for a home, but no one will ever find the home they are really looking for. Home is where the creator is and the creator is a higher source.

The ego copies heaven and pretends to give you a home. However, instead of warmth, you find a house with a war of lies, resentments and jealousy. There is nothing like home, which is the only thing the ego has ever spoken correctly. You always agree on that because part of you remembers heaven, your real home.

The realm of the higher source is holy. When you turn from the ego, you come upon reality where you are welcomed with the abundance of purity. Everything that belongs to you will return to you and you will soar to the highest place of your being where you can go toward time without end.

The higher source is life. It is being. Its doors are open for you to return home. It wants its children to return, and it waits. The source waits, but without impatience; impatience is of time and the source is not of time.

What is time to infinity? Only infinity is real. Every morning, every end of day, is an illusory dream state in which the mind is fascinated. Use time to restore your mind and remember reality. Whatever your eyes observe, you must heal. Heal the world to restore yourself. Heal the mind to heal the body. Heal all that you witness. The dream is to be well, which is a constant work, which you must do.

Your hard work consumes time, and it expires, not remembering creation while forsaking you. You probably are not aware of it, because your awareness is in the ongoing work of existence that you are doing. Even when it comes to providing thankfulness to a higher source for creating your everlasting love, you feel too tired and you would rather lie in the comforts of the dream.

Healing is not something you must do. Healing will undo something that is not well. Undo all learning that comes from the perceptive mind. Undo all judgment and undo the power you have given to the dream. Every passing road, every person you see or hear, every meal you eat and everything that you lay your hands on, deserves to be healed from their illusions. As much as you deserve a genuine moment, the world deserves the same, as a whole.

In the dream, humans think that alone they can walk to the plinth of creation. However, by isolating, they truly walk alone, for separation is the sphere of the ego. In its domain, the ego will leave them alone in the dark to die.

If you see the purity in a person, an animal or anything of body or form, adjoin with him in the light. If you only see humankind in your kin and not light, you reinforce the ego and that will guide you not to the realm of a higher source.

Some people think that by excluding themselves from the world, they will find enlightenment. You cannot be enlightened unless you see the light in others and you share the light with the world. When you see the light in others, you become aware of the light in you.

The light does not come from above, nor does it come from anywhere but from within you. You are the light and you are the darkness. Do not expect anything from the world to enlighten you. There is no light in the dark, for darkness is the lack of light. Accept your light-mind in order to be enlightened.

Humanity thinks it has many problems; wherever it is, there are numerous problems. The world is a problem. Even when you are close to a solution, the problem stays with you. Sometimes you think there is nothing for you to do; you think of yourself as useless before the problems of the world and the conflicts in your mind. You then refer to someone for help.

Only, that person is in his or her own conflict and conflicted minds cannot resolve conflict. You can never be free of conflict if you settle on the dream. Conflict is the ego's favorite pastime. If you give your problems to a person to solve, you can be sure that he or she does not know what to do. How could humankind solve the problem that it makes?"

A painter without water can add to the colors to his pallet but he cannot clean the pallet.

"As does everyone in the dream, you suppose it is not possible to know all. You follow the scheme that 'others know better,' and that only they can resolve what is in you. The ego-mind wants to avert from curing the conditions in which you are. It does not want you to see that your own mind has the power to resolve and release everything that it is choosing to keep. The people that you assume know more than you, are in their ego and so they know as little as you do.

Your spirit knows the answer to everything. It knows of no conflict so it clears what it knows not. It is the only one to solve all problems, as big as they may seem to be. However, it is your faith that lets it provide. It is your invitation to your mind that brings its presence.

Humankind promises every sort of cure and resolution to problems but nothing works because you are the one who sees the difficulty of the problems. When you choose to change what is in your thoughts you can resolve what is troubling you. You rely on levels and dimensions and consider a different scope for each problem. The problems appear to be of different magnitudes because you give more value to them based on your inner preference. In reality, every problem or conflict is simply a lack of light, and light is love. Your spirit resolves any problem by shining a higher source's love on you and on whom you ask for.

If you do not have faith in the one who knows, how can you trust something that does not know? Anything that you ask of your spirit, it will resolve for you. Your spirit clears the path for you. What you think is impossible will happen. What is of no good for you will disappear. Your spirit brings you to the realm of no pain and no preoccupations.

Never think your spirit will not solve a problem, relating it to the mundane. Everything in the world of form has a spirit as well, and your spirit knows its piety. In the present, where your spirit is, there is nothing to mend. What you see in time is already a memory. Spirit restores by shining itself on memories and by bringing the mind to presence.

The limitations of the body's eyes are so incredible, and yet you consider yourself as lucky because you can look at the forms that bind you to death. The ego made the body with eyes to view wrongdoing. You distinguish a world of form but cannot see what the object or the person really is. You see what you want to see, and everyone has their own meaning of what they perceive. What is true is unchangeable; therefore there is nothing correct in the world of perceptions.

No one can ever give a correct answer to your conflicted thoughts. Can there be a right answer when everyone sees his or her own judgments? When you are in a situation, and every occasion brings a new situation, you make your own opinion of what takes place. You measure the situation from what you learned from the past. The real meaning of every situation is lost in your own interpretation of the situation.

You value what is meaningful to you. When the meaning has changed, the value is lost. When you lose the value, the meaning is changed. When you are deceived, wl at was a meaningful change and what seems valuable gets lost.

When you are disappointed, you leave behind what has turned you down and you turn to something else with *hope. The ego will always deceive you for it does not want you to find what you are looking for. When you know what you are actually looking for is your truth, and when you accept that humankind will never have anything real to give, you will never rely on anything from the dream again. You will put your faith in yourself. You will continue to exist in the dream, not with hopes and fall downs, but with ease and certainty.*

Who knows better of your needs and of what is best than yourself? Be yourself. In you is where a higher source is.

Give no value to what you perceive. All in form will perish, no matter how much you try to keep it with you. How do you expect to keep anything forever if your body gets weary and then dies? You wish for infinite youth and you fight at odds to keep the body young. Nevertheless, no matter what you do, the body will get old. If your body will deceive you by descending to non-existence, how could humankind not deceive you? Only a higher source will not deceive you because its child is its truth.

Your imagination is infinite. You can assume what you want and make yourself believe anything. When you look at something, you can name it many different ways, but you only give a meaning that is more suitable for you. That is why without your judgment, what you think 'is' is not. Nothing really is until you make it real to you. If you have the power to make yourself believe that a dream is real and what you look at is real, then you can also believe that it is not real.

Only you cannot believe that two opposites are real. Only one is real: form or spirit. Look within your heart and see what you really value and what is meaningful to you. If you value form, you justify loss. If you value a higher source, which did create you and gave you life, then see the purity of everyone in the world and know that humanity's form, and yours, are not of reality."

Chapter Twenty-Three

Glory is absolute. It is something humankind cannot yet understand and cannot identify with. Glory is unexplainable because words are limited and whatever words could say about glory, they will never give the real meaning of it.

"You have not felt glory when you are in the ego, and that is why you can never understand what glory really is. When you liberate yourself from the identity of your body, you will experience glory, and you will know what takes place in the realm of creation. However, you will not recognize glory for as long as you think you do not deserve the glory of the creator.

Glory is not sitting in a corner of a temple. It is in you, in the temple of your mind. Listen to other men talk of glory. If anyone could recognize glory, his or her awareness would be with creation. If a person knows reality, he or she would not condemn you as a sinner. If anyone speaks of a higher source and bears in mind sin, he is speaking of the illusions of the world. If anyone regards you as deprived from glory, he does not know a higher source.

Glory is not a word, it is not a prayer; it is your truth. Say a prayer to your kin whose minds sleep as yours and who miss the moment of the glorious dance and songs that are in heaven.

Pray to your spirit to shine its light onto the world so it can restore the remembrance of reality and show their mind the way to the garden of infinite love. Pray not for the body of your kin but for their mind to remember who they really are. Pray to your spirit, for it is the one who listens to your words, and is the only one who can understand what your words say. Pray for the heart of humankind that is confused.

Your spirit made a promise to your creator to always care for you and be with you in every moment of the dream state. Your spirit reminds you of your reality; it whispers truth into your heart; it calms you when you despair; and it guides you when you stray. Your spirit is in you, waiting for you to call on it. If you ask it to lead you through the dream, your world will become abundant in joy. When your spirit responds it makes sure that everyone around you is in peace. It does not take the joy of others to give it to you. Your spirit shines truth in all.

If you want a joyful existence, if you want what you desire, will it to your spirit. It gives to you what is best for you. Ask it to show you love and to help you share love with the world, because love is all there is and love is what heals the treacherous intentions of the ego-mind. Your spirit always listens, even if the mind thinks it does not.

If you truly want love, if you want truth and if you want to be in a world of peace, then let go of the ego's plan for you to follow the dream. The dream does not understand deliverance. The rules of deliverance that humankind follows are false. The only deliverance that there is, is the correction from the ego-mind to the supreme mind.

You cannot trust what you do not know. The ego directs you wrongly. Why would it have an interest to direct you rightly if it does not want what is best for you? It does not care for you as long as it maintains its continuity and keeps you under its control.

The supreme mind is united. When you ask for your spirit, the supreme mind of the world listens to the call and responds with love."

The world that we witness is the form of an ego-mind. Therefore, what we see has a mind of its own. The bear would attack you only because it knows in its mind that you are afraid of it, and you know in your mind what the bear is going to do. The power of the mind is beyond the perceptive mind's comprehension. Every thought manifests, even if it seems like an insignificant thought. If you are in misery, that is how your mind wanted it to be.

"The considerate thoughts of what you see are just a delicate mask that covers the ego's intention to divide and destroy. Behind the innocence is guilt, and along with the guilt is fear, which is after every mind-asleep. If you put your expectations in the dream, be certain that nothing will conclude and nothing will show truth. The ego is always conflicted and forever lost.

Every circumstance in which you find yourself has been a projection of your mind. There is no reason to blame a higher source for your circumstances. The ego has given you everything, from where you are to how you are. It has given you the world that you have. It has guided you to the situations where you find yourself now; and you have followed your decisions all along.

The mind does not stop. The mind is always thinking. That is why there is no freedom in the ego-mind. Sometimes you think that nothing is working for you and that everything is against you. In the mind, there is no conflict but your own conflict. Your thoughts about other people do not do anything to them, but to yourself since your thoughts come from you and stay within you. No one can change anything for you unless you decide to change the circumstances by thinking differently.

In the mind, many thoughts come one after the other. Thus, you only recognize the one thought that you feel in the moment. When you are not able to get a thought out of your mind, you are still keeping it. This is the root of the pain and sorrow humans feel.

You choose to keep the thought or the memory that causes your discomfort. You are the only one who can accept and keep the cause and the effect of your thoughts; therefore, you are responsible for everything that you feel. You keep what you value and you value what you love. Remember the jewelry box. The box is your mind and the jewels are your thoughts. The ego will not let you accept your own responsibility. It keeps you away from your own truth. When you dig into the root of your thoughts and take responsibility for everything that you feel, pain will be forever gone.

You cannot do anything to save anyone from his or her pain and no one can do it for you. It is your own decision to feel pain and it is your own decision to release it. You can disassociate from pain. You cannot see that you choose to feel pain because in its cleverness, the ego put a world outside of you for you to place the cause of everything that you feel, and everything that happens to you. The answer and the end of pain are in your hands, yet there is guilt in you. Guilt is what does not let you be completely free of pain and grief. You keep memories that cause you pain to compensate for the guilt.

The mind in veracity is free from thoughts of distress. Thoughts that cause depression and concerns are only of the ego-mind. In holiness, the mind reigns and the body is a ray of light that is shaped only by the thought of love. If you are tired of pain, why would you want to remain in misery? Why keep resentful thoughts?

When you associate with the sorrows and the misery of the world of form, you feel responsible to share what goes on. The world makes you feel guilty for not joining in alliance with its suffering. You then feel uncaring and insensitive. In the world of the ego, there is no such thing as freedom of mind from objecting to pain. If you believe in the world of suffering, you do not believe in the world of spirit. Respond no more to humankind's pain. Respond to your higher source.

No one is guilty of anything. The mind assumes guilt but no one is at fault. The child of a higher source fell to sleep then became humankind, which is all this is. If you do not love the pain that you have endured for so many years, if you really do not love it, then do not keep the thoughts that cause pain. Do not hold on to memories that are illusions.

When you choose differently by asking your spirit to exchange your thoughts for love, the sadness and all of what you feel will be gone. You are terrified of the power of your own mind, of yourself. For so long, you have been choosing the ego and you have let it step on you with its fear and guilt."

Liliana: "Antoine, for so long I felt as though I was drowning in search of myself. Now I feel as though I am breathing for the first time."

"The variety of thought estranges the world. When you dwell in the ego's thought wave, you are not only battling with your own thoughts; but with the thought of others as well. What others think is also in you and from the thoughts that you receive, you keep the thoughts that you agree with. That is why your emotions are like rippling circles on a pond that resemble every passing event of your existence."

Liliana is curious to experience the recognition of a higher source. She wonders how she would feel and how she would see the world once she does.

Antoine: "When you recognize a higher source it feels so good. You walk with power. You feel that nothing can defeat you, even in form. You feel like almost floating but with a supreme control."

Liliana: "Can I go to the creator and say that I love Him?"

Antoine: "We don't need to do that. Your truth is His love."

Chapter Twenty-Four

Antoine and Liliana take a trip to Jamaica. Even though it is a vacation, she takes her notebook along. Location is irrelevant to the voice. Its work with Liliana is in a state beyond time and space.

On the white-sandy beach, Antoine rents a sailboat. He sails far from the shore until it is barely visible. With the hot sun and the crystal-like turquoise water, Liliana relaxes. The concept that everything and everyone has a mind fills her awareness. She feels as though she has joined her mind with the ebb and flow of the ocean. She becomes one with it and everything else fades and starts disappearing. The people on the beach, the places she has been, even her body and the sailboat itself evaporate from her mind.

"Some people in the world believe that holiness is the abstinence from sin; therefore, for anyone to be holy, he cannot have committed any sin. However, the belief in sin is of the dream. A world that sees sin is a world of sin. If a man thinks he is holy and judges others as sinner, he is recognizing sin, and what he recognizes is what he is. If anyone thinks that by addressing holiness, he is holier than

others, he is discriminating. Holiness is welcoming purity in everything and seeing the world of hate and death transform into a sinless and genuine world. Holiness does not mean exclusion from sinners. Holiness is to be one with all in the supreme mind.

The 'id' approaches holiness by evaluating people. It places behavior on a balance and justifies every act as sinful or not. As the mind projects comparisons, it separates. The world still does not comprehend holiness the same way that holiness cannot understand the concept of sin in the world.

When the mind accepts the body, it assumes that holiness means no wrongdoing. Who judges right or wrong but the mind itself? In reality there is no right or wrong. Sin is an idea the world inherited throughout many generations. Moreover, with no coherent reason of why the idea passed, the world has carried the burden of sin all along. Instead of judging a person for his or her actions, liberate them from the notion of their body, which is what defines sin. Liberate the world from the thought of sin so you can liberate yourself from the ideas of sin.

You have a mask on and from the concept of time, you have witnessed the world through the eyes of that mask. Now, in this moment, you can remove the mask and reveal the holy child within you."

There is something about her grandmother that makes Liliana think that she is ready to pass on, but she still remains in this world. Antoine tells her that grandma has already made her decision.

Antoine: "At that age, the mind is ready to go. It is easier for the mind to renounce the body when the body is no longer vital. When you look at your body and see it old, and at the same time you see the ones that are young and you cannot commingle with them, the mind becomes disillusioned."

Liliana: "But there is no way to reverse that. The body gets old no matter what."

Antoine: "If she knows that she is a mind, she will keep herself young regardless of how her flesh looks. But the mind that identifies itself merely with the body, prepares for isolation until death."

"Death happens in the world of form but it is not reality. Your reality is a mind, and a mind lives forever. Death can only be real for as long as you identify with the body. If you accept reality, there will be no relationships with death. Why is it difficult to renounce the idea of death? Why not just remove the mask and see the world through reality?

Do not hate humankind. Do not hate the ego. When you hate, you accept the ego.

How can you hate something when it is in you? This is why the mind is confused between hate and love. If you love someone and at the same time you hate another, then you are in the mind of duality. If you can have the capacity to hate, you are not in the mind of love. You can escape the thoughts of hate by turning to the mind of love.

To be free is to heal. To heal is to exchange judgment for your spirit. Holiness is now. Every now is a timeless moment with no past and no judgment. When there is no past, there is no sin. In a sinless world, you find truth."

The judge convicts the criminal for an offense. Nevertheless, in his mind, the judge can choose to see the mind of the criminal as a pure mind, as himself. The judge will do his job in the courtroom. With his thoughts, the judge can ask his spirit to shine light on the criminal's mind. Here is an example of a forgiving world. In their world, they have differences about each other and they follow the laws. In their supreme mind, they are forever one in peace and share a higher source's love.

"The world is as painful and horrible as you want it to be, as you choose the world to be. Who sees the world but your eyes, and what responds to what you see if not your mind?

Disengaging from the ego teaches forgiveness. To disengage is to heal the memories and to be in presence. In the present, the heart is forgiven because there is nothing to forgive. In presence, you teach that the world has never sinned. Moreover, to those whom you cannot teach with your words, because of the distance in the world, you can join with their mind by accepting your spirit in both.

The world will return to the realm of creation. Eventually, the child will remember his truth, but when and how is of no concern. If a kin wants to accept and stay in the dream of death, then it is his choice. Bless his heart and continue your journey to deliverance. You are not responsible for anyone's misery and sickness, as no one is responsible for yours. If a person decides to believe in the dream, he would be choosing death as you would be choosing life. If you dearly care for him, ask your spirit to help him change his mind about his mind so that he does not stay lost in darkness.

If you worry about someone in the world, you worry about yourself.

Whom you worry about will start searching for his truth when he gets tired of suffering. You might think it will be a long time if it takes a hundred years for a mind to wake to the remembrance of its truth, because you still believe that time and distance is needed to join with the creator. Remember, time is elusive and finite.

In reality, there is no separation. The mind of everyone in the world has always been with you and you have always been with a higher source. If you choose deliverance, you will not desert those who choose to stay in their dream state. You will never leave anyone. How can you leave what is in your mind? One day, everyone will remember himself as you remember yourself when you accept truth.

The separation occurred when the child fell asleep; then, the mind-asleep split into millions of other minds. A higher source is one mind, one thought, with its child. The world will return to heaven when it remembers reality. The return to heaven is in the mind; it is when you close your eyes from darkness and let your mind open to the recognition of infinity.

Humankind believes that, according to certain rules, only certain people will attain deliverance. There are no restrictions to enter through the doors of heaven unless you choose not to. A creator will not come down to free you; it cannot come 'down.' There is no distance to a higher source. The only distance is to wake from the dream.

Can you go into the dreams of someone who sleeps? A higher source loves its child and when the child wakes, it will share all with its child.

The ego has made you assume that it is your higher source and it has made you bow to its ostentation. By making you believe that it replaced your creator, it enforces the plan of the covenant not to remember that you are creation.

The ego will not be completely gone even when the body is gone. Where will it go if it is a thought? To relinquish the ego, you need great vigilance. You need to be wary of every thought and of every emotion that comes across and realize that they all come from the ego. When you are in the ego, you cannot extend life.

Even as the ego pretends to replace a higher source, it fails. If it had not failed, why is the world still searching for truth? Why is everyone, regardless of their own principles and convictions, still questioning their deepest pain in their heart? When you know truth, there are no questions. Find the creator in you, and give up doubt from what you have learned.

When the ego made humankind, innocent and unknowing, it made it so that it would grow and learn from it. The mind then stayed lost in a body, in a world in which it has to defend itself and others. Throughout your body's existence, you have only known what you have discovered. You suppose you learned a lot, but that understanding is very limited to only what the mind holds. The mind without form is lost, as you would feel exposed and vulnerable as if you were naked. If you could see the ego-mind, far from the awareness, you would view an insignificant nonbeing that laughs at your tears."

Sometimes we say that our memories haunt us, so we go from one memory to the other to try to forget the memory that we do not want. We think the sunny days make us forget the stormy ones, or that one body can make us forget another. Nothing of what we do can make us forget a memory.

Back from vacation, Liliana looks forward to a full night of sleep, but in the middle of the night, she wakes up. She remains alert, but then she finds that she cannot move. She is completely immobilized, paralyzed. She tries to call Antoine but she cannot talk. She tries to reach for Antoine but she cannot move. She uses all her force but she is incapable of doing anything. She panics but then pauses and says to herself, "This is not real and I will not accept it." She cries as she is released from what was freezing her. Antoine awakes and she huddles in his arms.

Liliana: "Why are these things happening to me?"

Antoine: "You are still afraid of love."

Liliana: "How can I be if all I want and all I give is love?"

Antoine: "I mean true love, love of the creator."

"In the mind, there is no replacement of memories just accumulations and storage of thoughts. For the house to be clean, you need to throw the garbage out, dust and scrub. For the mind to heal, you need to clean out the memories of the dream. There is no release of memories without your spirit.

Your spirit dispels every thought of suffering, pain and death in the mind. If you go to your unconsciousness, you can remember every experience. If it had not been for memory, you would not be able to identify with anything in the world. When you do not remember something, it is your choice not to want to remember.

If everything is in your mind, then the creator is in your mind. In addition, if you knew that the creator is in your mind, what do you think you would do about it? What would you do if you knew that the creator was so close to you? If you have been searching for your father and then you see him, would you not go running to his arms?

Your creator is not in front of you for you to run to it, it is within you. The games of suffering can be over and you can choose to see pain no more. You can release the conditions of the ego and remain in the dream with a forgiven mind abiding in peace. The effects of resentment and sickness will affect you only as you keep those ideas in your mind.

The ego will keep on projecting an external world. It will never stop making its many frightened screams for the mind to keep investing in the dream, and for the world to imagine a creator's punishment. Those screams are the horrors of the world that you consider out of your control. They are the situations from which you break down in terror at the sight of destruction. The catastrophes that you see are part of the master plan of the ego-mind. Do you really think your creator would commit such massacres? Would a creator do this to its children? The ego wants you to be afraid and to disbelieve.

In the world, nothing has ever changed. It is the same tragedy one after the other. Humankind keeps depending on the dream repeatedly. Look how much it has given you, look to all the things that it has for you. Alas, they all have been illusions and none of them have lasted. The ego has given you what you hold valuable, but the more it gives to you, the more time it steals from you. It gives you an idea of a world with things that you need in order to exist. It has also given you the conviction that with what it gives, you will be complete.

As you depend on time, the more you lose time the more anxious you become. The ego has put you in such a situation that you not only desire to have more than what you need, but as you struggle to get it, you fight against time. Since you bow to time, you do not even have time for yourself. You do not have time to think of where your thoughts are, and you do not have time to seek a higher source.

If you would stop for a moment, go into your mind and find your source. You will realize that this moment is real. What else is in your mind beyond thoughts of the past and beyond ideas that dwell in time?

The mind made time for you to get old, sick and die. You wish to stop time because you believe time is moving you forward. Time is memory. As long as you choose the ego, as long as you believe you are humankind and that the world of form is your reality, you will remain trapped in the illusion of time and you will never be able to find freedom of mind.

Pause for a moment and think beyond time. After the sun has set and before it sets again, has anything changed in your mind? You feel you have grown a day older. You suppose you have gotten some rest or that you have learned something new. However, what is in your mind has not changed. The thoughts that you choose to keep in your mind do not change no matter how many moonlights you see.

You are dreaming, and that dream is disappointing you. Think of one thing that is not of grief. Why would you want to stay in a dream where years of tears follow the tiny moments of joy? Renounce what the ego has given you and see only the purity of yourself and the world.

When a person is in grief, when you hear the devastating roar of the ego-mind, and you share the pain and the sorrow of those hurt, you are not sharing sympathy. You are only sharing illusions and making the ego real to all. Sympathy is not love and it is not caring. It is feeling sorry for yourself ensuring that you will be, and have been, in the misery that you see. Sympathy is the sorrow that you will die, like those you witness dying. Crying over death is damning the child of a higher source. It is accepting that your kin has died and that you will die. Sympathy for pain and death is giving power to the dream. It is saying that the ego has won.

If you really care for the world, then restore truth in every person that you meet. A lifeless body in the morgue is just the form that its ego-mind made. If you cry for the body, you are just crying for a form. The mind of whose body is dying is still in your mind, and it is up to you to accept either the ego-mind or the supreme mind. Which one you accept is who you really are. The same is for the people who move around you. Their mind is in you. Which one will you accept?"

Chapter Twenty-Five

The ego will be there with you for as long as you want the ego to exist. If you are in search of total freedom however, and if that is what you really want, then there is no more need to keep the ideas of the dream.

"Nothing of the dream will bring you freedom since freedom is of the mind. Have the moments of freedom in the body brought you any freedom of mind? Has the burden of your thoughts stayed with you? If you are free in the mind, nothing of the world can imprison you. What anyone does or says with their ego should have no effect on you. How could a vain action affect you when the ego is of no significance to you? In every moment, the world gives you the opportunity to select the ego or truth, whichever you choose, it will strengthen the power of the one that you choose. The more you choose the 'id', the more you dwell in it, and the more you depend on it. The more you choose truth, the more your awareness vivifies."

One or the other, we cannot maintain two families, not at the same time. How can we remain positive and at the same time remain negative? We cannot retain both attitudes simultaneously. We must choose.

If reality is in present tense, how can we also be in the past? As long as we are in the body, we are in the world of form. How real are you going to make the ego? If a person slaps you on the face, would you degrade yourself to his ego and respond, or would you instead deny his ego's existence and join with the power of heaven that is within your perpetrator?

"Men believe that they must defend themselves, otherwise they will lose; but the one who decides to stay in the ego is the one to lose. If you respond to someone who has slapped you in the face, you associate yourself with the ego. Furthermore, if you are within the realm of the ego, you lose your own peace of mind and self-control.

Do not fall into the trap of the ego. You have nothing to defend against anything or anyone, given that everything is unreal. If you want power, there is absolutely no need to side with the ideas of the unreal. Why side with the ego if ego is the fear of power? The more you do not accept the ego, the more powerful you become. It is your choice to accept all humankind as either ego or holy. If it is holy then you see no judgment, no meaning and no exceptions. If the hug of a friend is more special than the smile of a stranger to you, you are admitting the ego.

Either one should mean the same to you because both are no more than a chance to share love. Continue your existence in the world until the body goes, but be conscious of truth.

Maintain your faith; your spirit will make your path a better existence for you. When you have doubt about anything, you isolate by discarding the power and the light within you. How can you be alone when your spirit is always within you? But, if you choose the ego, your spirit can do nothing for you. However, it will wait until it hears the call from you. It is hard to have complete faith when you are in state of fear."

Liliana has acquired a keen sense of awareness of her "state of mind." Today she discerns that she is in the midst of a fear episode. She attempts to rise above the negative sensations, but to no avail. She tries to attain a sensation of peace, but her fear is actually too strong and evokes a feeling of extreme pain and convulsion. Her body begins to tighten and she finds that she cannot seem to recognize Antoine. Antoine tells her to go to her sacred spirit, but she has no control. He takes her hand in his, and it is not until then that she is finally able to calm down. After that, she felt numb and could not hear the voice in her. She felt weak and disappointed until she was finally able to again find the voice that lifts her from her hurting body. She is finally ready to be finished with her ego.

"Some people fear to have faith because they have experienced disappointment. In the dream, faith is belief. When there is belief, there are questions and expectations. Faith is unquestioned. The ego has failed, that is why there is no certainty in the world. It is hard to depend on anything or anyone. The world is lost and does not know what to believe in anymore. The eyes of the world have seen so much destruction that it has lost its trust, even to a higher source. Now you sit before the world that you see and you feel vulnerable fearing you may lose it all. You do not know what is to come as your existence shortens and moves toward its end. Some of you feel that you are at the borderline gasping for your last breath.

You are terrified at the rages of the ego. You sense that the world is going to end, that every form will perish after its given time, that nothing is forever even as new bodies and forms come into existence. Thus, as you still think that the world is immortal, you absorb the suffering of everyone and you keep misery within you. You bind yourself to desolation, which is where the ego wants you to be. The ego wants you to be in despair. It wants you to run from a higher source. It will take the little forms in different shapes that it offered you for a momentary state of happiness. The ego destroys as it pleases, for it does not care what is lost since it knows it has you under its control. The ego scares you with death, which should not scare you at all.

Are you afraid of dying? Then, change your ideas about your body and become your own mind.

If you accept the world of the ego as real, it will keep disappointing you until it destroys you. However, destruction is only of the dream. It is impossible to destroy the child of a higher source in you. If you accept that you are the holy child and that your truth is spirit-mind, then humankind's actions should not trouble you or affect you at all.

When you wake up in the morning, does it matter what happened in the dreams while you slept? The ego is the dream. It is not real, and whatever comes from the ego is not real, even to the point of its own destruction. If you want to choose a world of suffering and make destruction real, you value a short existence of grief.

Open your eyes to the world of forever and wake from the world of death. In infinity, nothing ends. The world of a higher source will never end; it is your real world. Follow what your spirit has for you. It will restore your reality and keep you saved from the horrors of the ego. It will restore your power and show you the truth behind everything that you see.

When you try something, and that something does not work, you then try something else. When you realize that what you thought would work did not work, you would then take another alternative. Ask yourself if the dream has worked for you. Look into your heart and answer yourself if what you trusted before has given you what you truly want. Do not make riches and status real to you. Has the dream given you the joy, the peace and the love that you want? Whichever your answer is, heaven knows that the ego has not given you what you want because the world is crying for what it has not. Humankind can only pretend to be satisfied with all the things it has.

You know that you are strong-willed. You know that when you do not get what you want, you go somewhere else to get what you want. Even when what you want is not much, you do not try to get it from something that has nothing to give. You are like a lavished little child since you are the child of a higher source; when you are with the creator you have everything.

Now when you are not with your creator, you may want "it" all. If what you want is all, and the ego has given you nothing, would you not go somewhere else to get "it" all? Be yourself, child of a higher source; go after all that you want. Just remember who has what you want. In the world, joy has the price of peace. If what you want is joy, be certain that you know that you have to pay the price with peace. Joy is nothing without peace. Forget about getting love from the ego. The ego does not even know the meaning of the word love. The word itself scares it and makes it disappear. People hover in circles in a constant search for love. Searching for love is their reality. If you want love, go to your mind and ask your spirit to unwrap the gift of love that a higher source has extended to you.

Since you were born, all you have known of is change. You have been navigating in a current of change. When someone does not give you love, what do you do? When you like something no more, what do you do? When something does not give you what you want, what do you do? You change, and you know how to change."

Liliana walks up the hill through the morning fog. There is a peaceful silence in her mind. Her body feels so light that she hardly feels the ground when she walks. She has no thoughts. She text-messages Antoine. "Thank you," she writes. Antoine replies, "For what?" Liliana writes back, "For showing me the light." Antoine replies, "Always thank your spirit and the creator. Thank yourself for accepting your truth."

"You always change what you think is not good for you. Then, change misery by choosing peace. Change sickness for love. Change death for infinity. Change the

ego for reality. Change humankind for the child of a higher source. You are a spirit, as you have always been. You are a consciousness that chooses, and you have a will. You can change as soon as you want. You can change whenever you want. You are the power of a higher source. The only difference is that a higher source knows who it is. You still think that you are something different, a body that is bound to pain and death. You are still in forgetfulness of who you are. When you know who you truly are, when you identify with a higher source, you will know how powerful you are. The power that the ego has to offer is the power it imposes over the world. But the power that you really are is the power that defeats the ego. That power is always there to protect you from the world of illusions.

The ego is not beautiful - quite the contrary. It plays a fairy tail, but at the first beam of the light, it turns back to its nothingness. How can anything be beautiful when it is dull and limited? What you see as beautiful you want to be beautiful. Humanity wants to see beauty; it uses landscapes to characterize beauty, but when it cries from pain and sorrow, nothing has any beauty. You seek beauty because it reminds you of reality. Beauty comes from the realm of truth.

What comes from a higher source has no limitations and no shades therefore it is indescribable. The ego is a monster that wears silky gowns and dances the waltz. With its fancy dresses, it puts a spell on you to distract you from the truth. If you really want to see beauty without a spell, your spirit shows it to you. Every noticed object will transform into a beauty so unique it can only express purity.

Unmask your ego. There is nothing beautiful in the world of form, only in the mind of a higher source. Beauty is perfection and only a creator is perfect. No body or form is perfect, so there is no true beauty in the body. Your beauty is your soul. See the light that surrounds all of humanity, and see the perfection of its surroundings. The world desires beauty, but no matter how people adorn their body with different garments, they still feel uncomfortable in their own skin. Humanity feels uncomfortable because the body is the opposite of the world's reality. You are beautiful. Nurture and continuously feed the spirit. If you exchange the ego-mind for the mind of light, the body will reflect pure beauty.

The ego thinks it can fool you forever but it is only fooling itself. It never thought that the power of heaven would unceasingly ask your spirit to remind you of your reality. The ego will do anything to confuse you more and make itself real to you. It does not want you to recognize your spirit since it only knows of itself. If you want to listen to truth and accept that you are the holy child of heaven, be honest with yourself and accept nothing that the dream offers you. Whenever you feel something, understand that the ego wants to separate you from your truth.

Pain, sickness and death are the manifestations of the ego-mind, the mind in fear. In addition, what you feel will carry on only for as long as you want to keep the thought of fear. If you question suffering, despair or misery, then open your mind and you will be able to find the source of all that. To find out where sorrow and death come from is your first step to freedom.

You are with the creator in your mind. You can still be in the body and think with a higher source. You should take care of the body and do what is necessary to maintain its existence. If you do not take care of it, if you hurt it or abandon it, you would be in accordance to the rules that the ego has for you. Decay and death are inevitable for the body, but if you invest in and accept what it feels, you would be investing in the ego and you would be ignoring reality. Everything that happens to humankind comes from the ego-mind.

The world is still afraid of a higher source. Every feeling is the projection of that fear. Every action is to hide the fear of death. When you see a dead leaf on the ground; w hen you see a rotten fruit; when you hear of a sick body and even when you see the sun set, the mind remembers death. Death is the reminder of the separation. It is the blame for having left a higher source.

In loving situations, a parent would not take the life of his child regardless of the circumstances, and no matter how severe. In addition, as so, the creator extended its life to you for you to be forever in infinity with it. It is you yourself in the ego-mind, which you yourself made; the one who decides when to die.

The ego-mind has gotten ahead of you. It comes and takes you away when it pleases and it makes the world believe that the cause of death is outside of you and out of your control. In your present time, as humankind, you suffer every given moment with the thought of death. Only what is in form will keep on dying for as long as you think of yourself as a limited body."

Liliana wants to be done with her ego. She asks Antoine how much longer it will take to make her transformation and what else she has to go through.

Antoine: "The mind is like an onion. The onion has layers and those layers are like our memories. To get to the core of the onion you have to peel layer by layer. If you just cut it in half, you only cut the core and the layers will remain there. The only way to get to the core is by peeling the layers. The same way with the mind: To get to the core, which is the higher source, you need to detach from the memories that keep you from going there, which are all part of the ego."

Chapter Twenty-Six

Is there a spirit or a soul that lives within every being?

"Many, at some point, have agreed that there is a spirit or a soul that lives within every being. Yet, some people say that spirit and body are apart and that it is a choice to be either spiritual or secular. Some people do not identify at all with the spirit because for them, the body means all. They believe nothing is more credible than what they can see, touch, feel, smell and hear.

Those who are bound to the body and simply believe in form think that the spirit is the unknown and unreachable; that the spirit is not within their comprehension to understand. Perhaps they get a sense of it. However, devotion to the body invests in guilt, and that will only bring grief and sickness. In that sense, they will be busy with their body and they would not even consider a thought about their spirit. For those who idolize the body and worship sickness, their spirit is not in harmony with their desires and needs.

Spirit-mind-soul is your reality: Spirit is when you are one with a higher source, with no dreams of form. Mind is the consciousness. It is the thought that fell to sleep, and it is the thought that made the ego-mind.

Your mind lives forever, as does your spirit. Your supreme mind is the mind that is always with creation. The ego-mind is the mind-asleep and will only exist for as long as you believe in the dream. The ego-mind seems to last forever in time it but it does not exist without your power; you enforce that power every moment you identify yourself with the body. Therefore, your identification with the body and the world of form binds you to death. Nothing can touch the child of a higher source. The child of heaven does not die.

The ego mind exists only in its dream state, and as humankind, it dies. Every body or form that you see is destined to die. Have you ever thought what remains after a person dies? Where did all the suffering and pain go? Did all the misery produce anything of value? If consciousness and thoughts are not of the body, where do they go once the body dies? What happens to thoughts if the thoughts are not form and only form can die?

Think beyond the body. Think realistically and honestly. If you are your thoughts, given that no one can think for you, then you can never die. In the ego-mind, you will keep the idea of death and you will keep on finding yourself as you are now: in scarcity, limitations, fear and sickness. In your supreme mind you are completely free. The body is nothing without a thought yet the thought never dies.

When death affects you, you accept death onto yourself and onto the world. Death is not a reality. The spirit cannot die. You have never died. You are not the same as a body and you will never die.

Death of humankind is unpreventable, and that is a fact. Understand that the only reason the ego made the body was to prevent you from remembering your immortality. Within the body, you will not recognize your reality and you will keep searching. The only way to live is to renounce death. Value the truth about yourself. Value that you are a spirit and that spirit is infinite. If you accepted your truth, what would death be to you?

Once you know that the body of your kin is no more than a form, which his ego made to distract him from the grace of creation, would you shed a tear over that body's death? Would you cry or suffer over the wretchedness of your kin's ego? Would you not rather join with him in his mind forever?

You are in constant fear of loss. You fear losing those who are significant to you and those you depend on. You fear being alone and being abandoned by the death of those you love. You fear being lonely because you remember the solitude you became when you left the realm of creation. You fear because the ego has made you think that you are weak and that you are alone in the earth and vulnerable to the madness that you see.

If you knew that you walked with the power of the higher source; that you were one with the world, would you still be afraid of being without the body that you cry for? When a person dies, you assume he or she has perished, so you cry. Instead of crying for the body, would you not say a prayer for the mind of that person to remember his reality? Pray for forgiveness and liberation from the concept of death. There is nothing to respect about death unless you honor the ego. Yet it is still hard for you to disallow to death.

You think of death because you believe in time, and every passing minute is a minute closer to death. Time enforces death; therefore it is your worst enemy. Thus, when you disown death you will find immortality.

You have a free will and that free will is not to choose between one form and another. Your free will is to choose between death and the creator. You fear and you desire both. You still desire and fear death; otherwise you would not accept that body that is set to die. You desire and fear the creator because it is your reality. You desire death because you are afraid of the creator. What you desire you get and what you get, you have desired. Only, in this case, you desire two opposites.

When you desire two opposites, you find yourself in conflict. That is why you might feel two forces pulling against you. One is the power of heaven, which is always there and is reality. The other is the power you give to the ego, which is the power against reality. If you pause and think, you would realize that everything you do is to avoid confrontation with both death and reality. You cannot avoid death; that is why you suffer now. You are terrified of a higher source; you think your creator is a monstrous being that will strike down your sins and sentence you to hell. A higher source, your real creator is not testing you and will never condemn you. It is abiding in your heart and all it wants is for you to acknowledge truth and to share with creation the love that it extends to you.

You have been lost; you do not know where to go. You want freedom but you are afraid of it. You want to live infinitely but you are still attracted to death. You say you love a higher source but you do not know where to find it and how to love it. How can you love something when you do not know where it is? Nothing in your mind is clear. You live in confusion because not even your 'reality' is clear to you. There are many stories of creation but they all lead to the same source.

Mind, spirit, soul, energy, light: They all come from one cause. No matter what you want to withstand as reality is always the same for all. The differences are only with how you interpret the world, and you interpret what you assume as knowing. The uncertainties of the world are unanswered.

You touch things and objects everywhere you go, but nothing is ever concrete. Dreams evaporate. Dreams get broken. You go from one wish to the other because no matter how much you have, you still do not get what you want. What you really want is reality; however, you cannot find your reality because when the ego promised you a paradise of love, you gave up the remembrance of yourself.

Your world is your mind but you are in the thoughts of the mind that is in darkness. That is why no thoughts are ever clear to you, nor are they clear to any other mind that drifts apart from truth. There is no certainty in the thoughts of the world. The world of the ego is the world of illusions, and illusions have nothing certain.

Where there is confusion, there is no peace. Confusion is not knowing and not knowing is fear. A higher source is truth, and peace is what a higher source has for you. Peace is not fear. Yet, what you know is fear since the body is an expression of fear. However, that fear is not real because the mind entered in fear when it fainted to sleep. Fear is of the dream and what is in dreams is not real. Your thoughts of death are of the mind that is not real. Therefore, your suffering is not real. Death and suffering are just illusions which the mind accepts to believe in.

Truth is certain and is very close; it is in your heart.

Either truth is real or the illusion is real. The truth abides in reality. The world seems to give you all, but it will never give you what you truly want. If it gives you what you truly want, it will be the end of the ego's existence. You think you want many things, but you really do not know what you want. In a state of fear, you cannot know what you really want. There are two candidates for what you desire: death or spirit. Which one do you want? Which one do you really want? You cannot have two opposites. You need to give up one for the other. Better yet, for your understanding: You need to sacrifice one for the other. If you want the spirit, that means that you will believe in death no more, you will see death no more, you will accept death no more and you will invest in death no more.

When you relate to death no more, you will find immortality because the ego is death. What you do not desire, you will not keep. What you desire you will not fear. What you fear you will not desire. In addition, what you know, you will not fear. Because you do not know that you know truth, and you think you know the ego, you desire *death. If you want no more of death, if you truly want to find your creator and never die again, ask your spirit to help you remember what you know. To remember a higher source is to fear it no more. It is to fear death no more and to think of death no more. The separation from the realm of creation is just the fear of remembering reality. That fear blinds, and what is untrue, you accept as true.*

The ego is just a thought, nothing more. What you see are just thoughts. You are a mind, and thoughts come from a mind. Yet, it is so hard for you to comprehend the truth, although it is very simple. The sorrows of the heart and the horrors of the world are nothing more than illusions. When humankind dies there will be nothing left.

The world exists in your imagination. It is in your mind. Nothing of what you see is real. Things are there, but they will vanish like the eyes that witness their form. How real do you want to make what is not real? How much do you want to believe in illusions? How much do you want to suffer and how attached to death do you want to be? What you consider as real is a dream.

Child, the answer to your questions is in my voice. These words tell you the truth. I am not trying to convince you, there is nothing to convince to the mind that knows all. I am just telling you the story of the child of the creator who fell asleep. Your questions of life are never ending because they come from the mind that sleeps. You have never been alone. Heaven and all have always been listening to the calls of your heart. The light may seem bright but that is because the mind has been in darkness."

What the eyes have seen comes from the darkness, for even the rays of the sun are dark in comparison to the light of a higher source. When you enter heaven, you will recognize your home and you will fear nothing.

"Understand that it is just one thought against truth and that thought has taken many forms. The thought of fear is in everything that you see and that you feel. It is hard for you to see the thought of fear divided into many little thoughts because the mind is confused. In the confusion of the mind, you classify your thoughts according to how significant they are to you. In the meaning of your thoughts, you find your happiness and your misery. You are the one who chooses the thoughts in which you are drowning.

The meaning that a higher source has for all is the meaning of love. Therefore, what is not of love is false.

The thought of love is consistent and it never changes. However, you always have a different thought opposing serenity because you are not in the mind of love. You travel in time with your thoughts. You are amused with your thoughts, but none of them is part of your truth.

You believe your thoughts are only for, and of, your goodness, but in fact, your own thoughts are the cause of your pain and unhappiness. Every thought that you have, other then love, is against you. The thought of love is your real thought, the only thought that provides goodness to you.

Nothing of what you see as the world is the real world. Respond to the world with truth. To everything that you see, respond with love. Your world is who you are and who you are is what you give. Give and teach the love that is in you. Remember that the whole world is in your mind. What you say and what you see is who you are. Question no more of what fear is, and whether or not you are in guilt. If you are not with the realm of creation, in guilt is where you are. Correct the error. You are the mind that made what you see. You are the one that has given the meaning to all.

The power to see no more pain and no more death is in you. Death is every form in the ego, every thought of sickness and every thing that you have known.

Have faith in your spirit. It teaches you the real thought. It erases every thought of death that is in the mind. You will see the truth within all of humankind through your supreme mind. You are a mind. That is why you are what you think. The body is just an interpretation of your thoughts, of who you really are. If you say that you want to live, hold your thoughts now and correct your mind from the ideas of death.

This message is just the beginning of how to understand the truth. There is much to say even though what is to say is meaningless to the truth. However, you are in a state of forgetfulness. Your mind is in darkness and you are confused. You believe in form and I need to communicate with you with what you know and with what you are familiar. The ego has taught the wrong truth and it has fooled you with its word. You believe in truth but you do not know what truth is because there are different truths in the world. The real truthful way is through your heart and when you know the real truth, you will know. At this point, you still need guidance to find your heart and remember how to listen to it. That is why spirit comes to you to teach you how to follow your heart and to help you understand that the ego is not your heart.

You know that the fire burns because it has burned you and so you will never go near the fire again. You would not go near the fire unless you wanted to be burned. When you know the truth, you will not go near the ego again; you will know what the ego is. The ego does not just burn, it destroys and kills. If you go back to the ego, it would only be because you are still fascinated with pain and you relate to death. Knowing knows, it does not believe.

If you believe, it means that you do not know. I do not want you to believe. I want you to remember what you know. You have said many times that you are tired of the sameness. You are tired because the world does not get any better no matter where you turn or what you do. Be sure that it will never get better, for the world is selfish and when the ego thinks about itself, it only wants what it desires. Sickness, pain, fear and destruction are what please the ego the most. You now have a chance to escape from that world, and that is to accept my words of love and ask your spirit to restore what you know.

Learning to know the truth is the acceptance of the understanding. Imposing what you know does not mean to learn. Truth is very simple, but what the mind has made is a chaotic world in madness, and that is what you have to learn about to unfold the truth. You have been with the ego time after time, and you know that everything that it has to offer has nothing of goodness.

Would you like to know more about the dream? You should understand by now that it will never bring you completion because totality is of the creator. Joy and peace is far from the agenda of the ego, because that is what you gave up when you accepted the ego.

The choice is always your free will. Nothing can hurt you except that to which you may give your power.

Patience: Be patient and pace yourself as you learn. What isolates you, use it now to unite with creation.

It is true, that the child cannot suddenly waken while it dreams. The child wakes up softly to avoid being frightened. The waking of the mind needs to be gentle.

The light of heaven will blind the ego and the power of the truth will break it down. You still cannot imagine the power of a higher source because the imagination of humankind is limited. What does the ego-mind know of power if it is powerless? Take time now and heal.

Heal the memories that are a burden to you and that hinder your peace. Heal the thoughts that keep you separated from your family. You believe in family. You believe in being loyal to your family. Accept then your true family and be with them. You will find full happiness and you will never be alone again. Your family loves you, and they are awaiting your return. Dreams have never been good to you and they never will be. A nightmare is a nightmare; it will never turn into a happy dream. Heaven is your home, and there you will find a perfect family where all is love and all is sharing.

Humankind deems that total happiness and freedom of conflict is boring. Humanity always finds something to do otherwise it gets bored. The ego wants you to feel bored so you invest more into its deceptions. It makes thoughts and desires for you to be restless and to busy yourself. It gives you the notion that it is entertaining you, yet it is keeping you from remembering yourself. People think that by doing what they desire, they will find joy. No matter what they do, though, they will still be bored because the ego is boring and has no joy. Can you see the merry-go-round of the ego? It makes you do, and as you invest in the doing, you get tired, and when you get tired you feel bored, and then you go and do more.

The ego is ingenious. It knows what it wants from you and how to get it. It knows how to protect itself from losing the power that you granted it. Do not let the ego scare you. Be vigilant. Be consistent. Be strong. Be faithful to your desire. Be loyal to the principal that you choose, the ego or your spirit. Be certain of what you want, to die or to live. Be yourself. You will learn the truth, you will learn of your power and you will become your power.

This message will soon close; it does not mean that the unfolding of the truth will end. There are many, many things to say for you to understand the illusions of the mind and to accept your truth. Communicating with you is simple, but your mind may be very confused. Ask your spirit, in your heart, to confirm reality to you.

In infinity, a higher source is within all as I am with you. Speaking to your mind with these words is the promise I have made and kept, in giving you your spirit that will guide and protect you from a vagrant ego, which is the persuasion of sin, and is what the world has always referred to as temptation.

Avoiding temptation does not mean avoiding the lures of flesh; it refers to the understanding of illusion. Your spirit does not judge your familiarization with temptations. Your spirit cannot see temptation. It shines its light, which will distance the ego from your path. It reminds you of who you are; that you will not be seduced with illusions.

Falling into temptation is having faith in something other than the higher source; and the dream is not of a higher source.

The birds are singing in paradise. They sing for your mind to wake. Gently open your eyes and see the rays of the bright awakening. The quavering dreams are not real. The thought of death is just an illusion. Deliverance is here, a higher source will not judge you. Your creator wants you to know that you are its child and that its love is yours. It is extending its heart to you. Look into the light of your heart and see its light. Know that you are its child and that you have done nothing wrong.

The body is there until it perishes. It is not your truth, not your reality. Humankind exists in time, however time is just a thought, and with each second it is in the past, and therefore not real. You are a mind, but you are in the mind-asleep which contradicts the mind that is of your truth.

You are not to die. You are to live forever in abundance of love. Accept holiness and see the world of darkness transform into a pure ray of light. Sorrow will no longer be meaningful to you once you know that the choice is in you. Release the burden of memories that separate you from the truth and join with the world. Be in a hallowed world. Save the world to save yourself from the conditions of the ego.

Peace is not what you do with the body. Peace is you. It is what abides in you. Peace is what spirit wants you to recognize. Nothing can bring you peace but the acceptance that peace is in you and is you. If you think that you do not have peace, it is not because you cannot find it. It is because you are choosing not to adjoin with your truth. You will find peace not in the identity of the illusions but in the pure child within you.

Say goodbye to suffering, it is not a part of you. Do not think of tomorrow; tomorrow and the previous second is not here. Here is now: present, where all is you. Heaven is your mind and you are in heaven now. The realm of creation is open for you. See with your mind and enter with no fear and no guilt. This moment, in your heart, is your truth. You do not have to search anymore. Your heart is screaming for certainty, and you have walked a thousand worlds in search for the truth. I am giving you the truth with my most humble heart. I love you as much as the creator loves you. You are part of my heart, you are my heart, we are the creator's heart, and we are all one.

When the child returns home, no more guilt will he behold. He will realize the thought of guilt was just a fantasy and he will have fears no more. The realm of creation is waiting for your return. A higher source wants to communicate its love with its child. The dreams of evil, sorrow and death have been too long.

Listen to the angels waking you. See the light of the new day that never ends. A higher source created you to share itself with you in absolute joy, peace and love. You are a spirit that lives in the universe forever in infinity.

The worries, the sickness, the pain, the fears and the decayed bodies are just an illusion. They are thoughts of guilt for having turned away from creation. Remember your creator and see every minute you thought was real disappear like a breath into the wind. Your spirit is to be with you, as it has always been, to guide you through the journey back into the realm of creation. The spirit and the creator are you. Your holy family waits for you to remember heaven; and here I conclude the book that says nothing except for the truth."

Illustrations

ILLUSTRATION 2

"Choosing Between Ego/Mind-Asleep and the Self"

This illustration demonstrates the concept of change from the mind in darkness to the light-mind: the mind of truth. The room has a light switch and a hand to turn the switch on. The brain has to think. That thought has to come from a source, which is the mind. In that sense, the brain functions in accordance with the mind. As we compare the room to the mind, the decision maker is comparable to the switch. Since the hand is part of the body, it takes orders from the brain, and the hand complies willingly. Therefore, for the will to activate, the mind would be our consciousness.

When we walk into a dark room for the first time, we are apprehensive because we cannot see. Similarly, when we split from the source, we enter the ego-mind which is darkness. The only way to move the mind away from darkness is to make the decision to turn to the light-mind. As in the room, we use the hand to turn the switch on, so there is light.

The room can only be light or dark. That is how our mind works. The mind cannot fragment into two different thought systems that function simultaneously. If we are in the light-mind, we have only one thought, the thought of truth. If we are in the mind-asleep, we have many thoughts, the thoughts of illusions.

We seem to have many thoughts at the same time, but in truth, we can only have one thought at a time. When we look at a painting, we seem to be looking at the whole landscape but we need to withdraw our attention from one object to be able to look at the other.

When we choose the light-mind, it shines through the darkness of the ego-mind and dispels it completely. That truth represents the consistency of peace, love and joy. On the other hand, when we choose the ego-mind or the mind-asleep we deny the totality of creation.

Body = Vehicle

Enlightened Mind = Sanity, Happiness...

Ego / Mind-Asleep = Insanity, Anger...

ILLUSTRATION 3

"Mind and Body"

This illustration represents the body and how it functions in response to the mind in which we choose to dwell. In illustration 1, we see the mind of a child who chose to split from the mind of the creator. The child made the ego-mind and the ego-mind made the body. Therefore, the body itself without the mind has no thoughts or life.

The body without a mind is like a car running in the neutral position. It runs but cannot move unless there is a driver to put it in gear. The driver then resembles the mind. The engine of the car is comparable to the heart of the body; the electronic panel to the brain; the oil to the blood and the gas to the food. The car needs maintenance in order to function. The car is just as the body, it needs care to maintain a healthy shell just as the body needs nourishment.

Basically there are two kinds of drivers: sane and insane. Within this illustration, we compare the sane driver to the light-mind and the insane driver to the ego-mind. Now, if the driver is the light-mind, we can be sure it will know how to drive skillfully. The body then, guided by the light-mind, is in complete joy, peace, health and sanity. On the other hand, if the driver is the ego-mind, the mind in darkness and fear, it will not know where to go and where to

A6

turn. It will be like an insane driver, driving insanely until it crashes. The body guided by the ego-mind is in sickness, depression, anger, misery and sadness until death.

If we compare the driver to the consciousness of our mind, the driver has a choice to be in the light-mind or the ego-mind. The decision will depend on how we choose to drive the car, just as it is our decision how we want our bodies to exist. It is up to us to choose which thought system to dwell within, otherwise the mind is at odds between the two thought systems: sanity, which is the light-mind or insanity, which is the ego-mind.

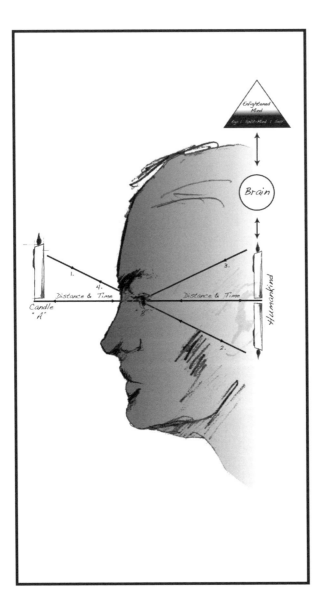

A9

ILLUSTRATION 4

"Perception, Memory, Past."

This illustration refers to the laws of physics. When the ego-mind made the body, it included senses to keep us comfortable, seemingly in control and amused in order to appear real (as an illusion.) Yet, the body is not real. It is obvious that our so-called senses are touch, sight, hearing, taste, and smell; each nerve travels to the brain and the body reacts. However, the brain does not work without the mind. Without the mind, the body and the brain are lifeless.

Let us give the example of perception since all senses work in the same manner. Consider the eye mechanism. The Laws of Newton state that if there is a distance between the eye and an object, distance can be stated in intervals of time. When an object travels from point A to point B it has a distance to travel between points measured in time. There is distance and time when the object goes from its position (point A) into the eye (point B.) Once the image enters the eye, the image travels to the brain to be registered. However, in order for the brain to respond, the brain must assimilate the image in the mind in order to identify it. As a result, the image will stay in the mind as a memory. It will stay there with every image that we have ever perceived. Once the image is recognized as a memory and it is identified by the mind, the mind transmits the meaning to the brain. The brain projects the image back through the eye, perceives it as separate, and makes a judgment.

It is understood that time has passed during the recognition and the reversion of the image. In that sense, the perceived object becomes the past. We do not think it is the past because the mind is extremely fast and it is continuously sending recognition signals back and forth to the brain. The constant response of all our senses makes us believe that we are operating in the present, but in fact, if there is distance and there is time elapsing, we cannot be in the present. The only way to be in the present is if there is no past.

What seems to be far away exists within our memories. Our memory dwells in time. Time is an opposition to the infinite. The infinite is reality.

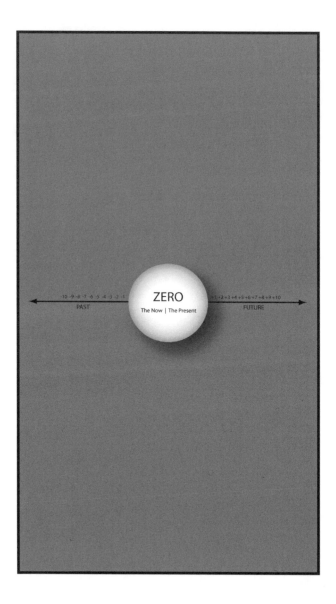

ILLUSTRATION 5
"Present"

The present in this illustration is timeless. The present existed before time existed, as it will be present when there is no more time. The present is infinite. The ego-mind added the past and the future to confuse us. The present, illustrated as "zero," is a void of negatives and positives, or of the past (memories) and the future (anticipation.)

In this illustration: from zero, subtract one and you will remember the past; and from zero, add one and you will think of what is ahead or anticipate the future. If you know that the present is real, then neither the past nor the future is present, therefore not real.

If we add minus one and plus one we get zero. If you bring (add) the past into the future, you do not have anything, though mathematically it is zero, it is just thinking. "Minus" or "Add" from either side of zero is only speculation, nothing is real when you agree that only the present is real.

Here is an example: When you meet a person for the first time, you get an image from ears (sound,) hands (touch,) or your eyes (sight) to your brain (which controls the senses), then consequently the mind. You then process or assimilate what you hear, touch or see, and symbolically identify images; this is 'zero minus one', which is the past (or memories.) When you converse with this person for a date tomorrow, this would be 'zero plus one', which is the future (anticipation.)

$$\text{``}\underline{0+1}\text{''} + \text{``}\underline{0-1}\text{''} = 0 \quad \textit{or} \quad \text{``}\underline{0-1}\text{''} + \text{``}\underline{0+1}\text{''} = 0$$

$$\lor \qquad \lor \qquad\qquad \lor \quad + \quad \lor$$

$$+1 \quad + \text{-}1 \quad = 0 \quad \textit{or} \quad \text{-}1 \quad + \quad +1 \quad = 0$$

The past determines the future so without a past there is no future. This is how the dynamics of the ego-mind function, from its memories. Without memories, there are no judgments, no classification and no identification. The body is continuously sensing and that makes it seem like we are in the present. The body grows from moment to moment in its various conditions and its various times. When we are of the body, it is impossible to be in the present for even more than a nanosecond. The future is always less than a second away. Within the body in the past, it is the same as zero minus one, which means we constantly respond to memories. In the present there is no time, therefore it is infinite *(ex: Alpha & Omega.)*

From zero to below zero, you will find memories or the past. That means that in the present, you will not find memories. Only in the present, where there are no memories of the past, and without association with the past or future, can we live in reality.

When we are in the light-mind (a mind you can remain in forever), its light shines onto the ego-mind and dispels its memories. You will see in the illustration of "Zero," that only the zero is static. As a result, in our mind, only the light-mind can eliminate the loyalty (meaning 'loyalty' to the ego-mind) from the past and the future. The light-mind can keep us in the present where infinity is immortality and reality. The light-mind is the supreme mind and we will not die.

Epilogue

As we conclude our narrative, we realize that it will be normal to question many of the concepts and statements conveyed in this book. If we have motivated you to ask such fundamental questions about how to discover truth, especially as it concerns human existence, then we have succeeded.

We urge each reader to open his or her mind and clarify the uncertainties that hold us back from gaining free access to our minds. As the voice told Liliana: "You can certainly trust your own spirit as to what is real." If the reader agrees that the message contained in this book is true, then the question of our spirituality cries out for further dialogue. Take heart. It is not over.

From the Authors,
Antoine Bacha and Liliana Franco

"Mind, Spirit, Soul, Energy, Light, they all come from one source. No matter what you want to accept as reality, is always the same for all."